D0742794

RENEWALS 458-4574

DATE DUE

GAYLORD			PRINTED IN U.S.A

WHOM THE GODS LOVE
The Life and Music of
GEORGE BUTTERWORTH

WHOM THE GODS LOVE
The Life and Music of
GEORGE BUTTERWORTH

MICHAEL BARLOW

Preface by
VERNON HANDLEY

TOCCATA
PRESS

To the memory of my parents

First published in 1997 by Toccata Press

© Michael Barlow, 1997

Music examples set by Jiří Kub

British Library Cataloguing-in-Publication Data
Barlow, Michael
    Whom the gods love: the life and music of George Butterworth.
    I. Title
    780.92

    ISBN 0 907 689 42 6
    ISBN 0 907 689 43 4 (pbk)

Typeset in 11/12½ pt Baskerville
by York House Typographic, London
Printed and bound by SRP, Exeter

Contents

List of Illustrations

George

So thou hast died for England! with thy 'boys'
Around thee. Sad and strange it seems to me
That thou should'st die this death, when peaceful joys,
Creative art, music and song, (for thee
Thy rightful heritage, and proper aim)
Were thine. Thy country called thee! Age to man,
And beast, a faithful friend, to kill and maim
Was alien to thy kindly nature's plan.
'Whom the gods love, die young.' It must have been
Inferno to thy gentle soul! Hell's noise,
Such frightful sounds, and sights, the world's ne'er seen!
But, borne aloft on Death's soft, sable wing,
Thou hearest, *now*, the Heavenly Voices sing.

'In Memorian G. S. K. B.', by 'M. E. B.', 13 August 1916

George Butterworth, photographed in Leeds in 1913
(courtesy of the English Folk Dance and Song Society)

PREFACE
Vernon Handley

Art criticism has always been at pains to keep artists firmly in categories: great, important, influential, minor. The exercise has its uses, especially for students of art history – but the more music one hears, the less useful the two extremes in this list seem to matter. As a performing artist, my mind during preparation for a concert is frequently invaded by music I am not about to perform; when I am resting, I am beset by such music. The invasion is not made by exclusively 'great' music; indeed, the interesting thing about it is that so much of it is by unfamiliar or 'minor' composers.

In the last twenty years I have conducted regularly in Scandinavia and Australia, taking care to play a good deal of the music of those regions, the works of lesser composers as well as those of the established masters. The experience I described above holds good: some of the lesser works and composers will not leave me alone. This pleasant itch is the good fortune of many who know the music of George Butterworth, and it yields to no lasting remedy.

The death of young artists in the First World War has been well documented, and what might be called the 'if only' factor exhaustively explored. Michael Barlow's study does something more valuable. It dwells on the positive and vigorous aspects of Butterworth's character, aspects not obviously suggested by the character and inspiration of his works. I say 'obviously' because many who comment on art glibly transfer the prevailing atmosphere in an artist's works to the artist as a person. Delius the young mountain-walker and older irascible is lost in the last cadence of the first cuckoo, as is the self-pity of Beethoven in the initial gesture of the finale of the Fifth Symphony. But is the message that the reflective idyll is weak and the obvious optimism strong? The former is accepted with more damage to the composer than the latter. Michael Barlow will give pause for thought to those who have seen Butterworth as merely a gentle dreamer.

It is as well to remember that in only a few years Butterworth's handful of works will have lasted as long as many of those accepted as masterpieces when he was born. He appeals to 'the more thinking among mankind'. To all those who are susceptible, his works leave a clear picture of the strength of his vision and inspiration. The character emerging in this book is an absorbing and almost formidable young man, and his emergence establishes a balance between the man and his music. I welcome the itch, and I know I am not alone.

Vernon Handley

INTRODUCTION

George Butterworth. Composer. Collector of folk songs. Morris Dancer. Cricketer. Soldier. [...] 'Great in what he achieved, greater still in what he promised.' No composer's reputation stands on so small an output [...]. It is in the truest sense *English* music.

So began a radio talk in 1942,[1] accompanied by a recording of the coda from Butterworth's finest work, the Rhapsody, *A Shropshire Lad*. Who was this versatile young man, killed in World War I at the age of 31? Relatively little is known about his life, and his surviving compositions are few, but eighty years later his music lives on, loved by musicians everywhere it is known.

Butterworth's early death was obviously a deep loss to his numerous friends in the musical world, and to English music itself. It would be foolish to consider what he might have achieved during a longer life, as it would with Mozart or Schubert; all who knew him agreed that his loss was severe. Michael Kennedy compares Butterworth's position to that of Elgar, if the latter had died in 1898 (at the age of 41, ten years older than Butterworth), 'leaving behind in *Froissart* and the *Serenade* [for strings], two works of accomplishment and even more promise'.[2] But what if Elgar had died in 1888? Certainly his output would have been far larger than Butterworth's but,

---

[1] *George Butterworth – The Man and His Music*, BBC Home Service, 14 July 1942. The BBC script gives no authorial attribution; the programme was devised by Elizabeth Poston and Roger Fiske, one of whom is likely to have written these words.

[2] *Portrait of Elgar*, Oxford University Press, London, 1968 (2nd edn. 1982, 3rd edn. 1987; issued by OUP as a Clarendon Press paperback in 1993), p. 46.

despite recent revivals of interest in Elgar's juvenilia, would not the quality of the younger composer's work stand apart from his? Is there no doubt as to whose music would survive the longer?

Many gifted men, from all walks of life, were victims of the War. Among Butterworth's friends were Bevis Ellis, who promoted concerts in London shortly before the War, and three fellow morris-dancers, George Wilkinson, Perceval Lucas and Reginald Tiddy. Other composers, full of promise, lost their lives: W. Denis Browne (1888–1915), Frederick Kelly (1881–1916) and Ernest Farrar (1885–1918) and Rudi Stephan (1887–1915).[3] Comparisons have been made between Butterworth and certain contemporary literary figures who met an early death, including Rupert Brooke (1887–1915), Wilfred Owen (1893–1918) and James Elroy Flecker (1884–1915), although Butterworth's colleague, the folksong collector Francis Jekyll, felt that Brooke 'might not have added to his reputation, whereas George was bound to go on increasing in power and independence'.[4]

Butterworth's output, even including the works known to have disappeared, is slender, and all his surviving pieces, with the exception of a song, to words by Shelley (*I fear thy kisses*),

---

[3] Browne, Kelly and Farrar, together with Butterworth, all showed signs of considerable ability as composers, of songs in particular. Browne was destined for a brilliant career, academically and musically (as composer, teacher, pianist and critic), and his nine surviving songs (outstanding among them *To Gratiana dancing and singing*) form the basis of his reputation. Kelly, an Australian, preceded Butterworth by a few years at Eton and Oxford; he wrote chamber and orchestral music, in addition to some two dozen songs, the early ones reminiscent of Frank Bridge, who was a close friend. He was also a concert pianist and a celebrated oarsman, rowing in the 1908 Olympics. Farrar, composer of fifteen songs and a considerable quantity of other music, was, like Kelly, a member of the Bridge circle, and is remembered today as an early teacher of Gerald Finzi. Stephan is considered a fore-runner of German Expressionism, and his music bears the influence of Delius.

[4] Letter to Butterworth's father, dated 16 August 1916; Sir Alexander Butterworth (compiler), *Scrapbook of Letters, etc. concerning George Butterworth, 1903–1922*, Bodleian MS Eng. misc. c. 453, f. 73.

and a number of the Housman settings, belong to the years 1910–14, although sketches for some of the existing works pre-date this period. John Rippin[5] suggests that Butterworth's work can be put into a better perspective when one considers three factors: first, the brief period of productivity that gave birth to his surviving compositions; second, his relatively late decision to follow music as a career; and third, the absence of any music from his last two years.

What, then, is Butterworth's position in the history of music, or, more specifically, in English musical history? His few works are, almost without exception, of a supremely musical character, revealing a truly indigenous style, liberated by and large from continental influences. This fact, in itself, was quite remarkable, considering the hold Wagner, Debussy and Brahms had on many English composers in the early years of the twentieth century.

Something of Butterworth's character will, I hope, be glimpsed in these pages: his modesty, his courage, his independent outlook on life. These and other facets gained him much respect throughout his life, whether from fellow undergraduates at Oxford or from former miners in the Durham Light Infantry. The tributes after his death were many; this one, from Reginald Lennard, an Oxford colleague, aptly sums up Butterworth's character:

> [He] hated shams of all kinds and humbled every impudent insincerity that he met. But for anything genuine, warm-hearted and courageous he had more than admiration, whether he found it on a village cricket field, or in a rustic public house, or in the mud of Flanders.[6]

---

[5] 'George Butterworth, 1885–1916: Part 2', *The Musical Times*, Vol. cvii, No. 1484, September 1966, p. 771 (the first part of Rippin's article appeared in the previous issue, No. 1483, August 1966, pp. 680–82).

[6] *George Butterworth 1885–1916 (Memorial Volume)*, York and London, 1918, p. 100. This was a private publication containing a memoir by R. O. Morris, Butterworth's War Diary, letters, appreciations and concert reviews; re-issued 1948, again for private circulation.

And this miniature portrait is from Hugh Allen, organist of
New College, Oxford, and later Director of the Royal College
of Music, in a letter to a friend:

> What a loss as a musician – and specially as a friend. His dear
> wayward manner, that friendly scowl, that tenderly gruff
> voice – all gone to pay a rotten debt to a bloody-minded lot of
> miscreants. And George, I'm sure, looking peacefully on
> somewhere.[7]

ACKNOWLEDGEMENTS

Assistance and information for this book have been forthcoming
from many different sources, and I wish to acknowledge my gratitude to a large number of individual people and institutions.

The following have been most helpful in many ways, and I should
like to thank them: Lionel Angus-Butterworth, the late Sir Thomas
Armstrong, Lance Baker, the late Sir Adrian Boult, the late Lady
Boult, Dr Vernon Butcher, Colin Butterworth, Michael Dawney,
John Dodd, David Dunhill, Paul Edwards, the late Sir Keith Falkner,
the late Joy Finzi, Lewis Foreman, Dr Ruth Gipps, Elizabeth Haigh,
David Healey, the late Douglas Kennedy, Stephen Lloyd, Susan
Murray, Wallace Southam, Madeleine Stephenson and Alan
Williams.

I would also like to extend my gratitude to the following institu-
tions: Aysgarth Preparatory School (and its Headmaster, Simon
Reynolds); the BBC Written Archives Centre at Caversham (in
particular Jacqueline Kavanagh); the Bodleian Library, Oxford; the
British Library; the British Music Information Centre; Dunstable
Library; the English Folk Dance and Song Society (and the staff in
the Vaughan Williams Memorial Library at Cecil Sharp House);
Eton College (especially Alastair Sampson, College Organist; Paul
Quarrie, College Librarian; and Penelope Hatfield, College Archi-
vist); the National Sound Archive; the North Yorkshire County
Library; Radley College (especially Robert Gower, Precentor, and
Tony Money, Honorary Secretary of the Radleian Society); the

---

[7] Quoted in Cyril Bailey, *Hugh Percy Allen*, Oxford University Press,
London, 1948, p. 139.

Royal College of Music; Trinity College, Oxford (in particular the librarian, Dennis Burden); and the University of Leeds, Brotherton Library.

My thanks are also due to the authors, publishers and copyright holders of all material quoted, both musical and textual: B. T. Batsford Ltd (Lewis Foreman's *From Parry to Britten*); Anton Bax (Sir Arnold Bax's autobiography, *Farewell, My Youth*); the BBC (BBC scripts and articles first published in *The Listener*); Cambridge University Press (Stephen Banfield's *Sensibility and English Song*); *Composer* magazine (article on C. W. Orr by Joseph T. Rawlins); Dr A. J. Croft (*Memorial Volume*, the Butterworth *Scrapbook* and unpublished scores in the Bodleian Library, Oxford; the scores include *Fantasia* for orchestra and Suite for string quartet); *English Dance and Song* (articles by Mike Heaney on 'Films from the Past', P. S. Heath-Coleman on 'Morris Dancing at Filkins', the late Frank Howes on 'Letters to Clive Carey', and the late Russell Wortley on 'The Bucknell Morris'); the English Folk Dance and Song Society (articles in *Folk Music Journal* by Michael Dawney on 'George Butterworth's Folk Music Manuscripts', the late Douglas Kennedy on 'Tradition', Derek Schofield on 'Revival of the Folk Dance: An Artistic Movement. The Background to the Founding of the English Folk Dance Society in 1911', and the late Russell Wortley and Michael Dawney on 'George Butterworth's Diary of Morris Dance Hunting'; also for articles in *Journal of the Folk-Song Society*; *The Ploughboy's Glory* (edited by Michael Dawney); and permission to reprint Butterworth's own article in *Journal of the English Folk-Dance Society* on 'The Songs and Dances in *A Midsummer Night's Dream* at the Savoy Theatre'); Ernst Eulenburg Ltd (Rhapsody, *A Shropshire Lad*, introduction by Sir Thomas Armstrong and music examples); Faber and Faber Ltd (Constant Lambert's *Music Ho!*); Hamish Hamilton Ltd (Sir Adrian Boult's autobiography, *My Own Trumpet*, and Michael Kennedy's *Adrian Boult*); Peter Kennedy (Maud Karpeles' *Cecil Sharp, His Life and Work*); Mrs C. M. Lloyd (BBC talk by her late husband, A. L. Lloyd, on *Folk Song and the Collectors*); *Music & Letters* (articles by Dr Vernon Butcher on 'A. E. Housman and the English Composer', and William White on 'A. E. Housman and Music'; letter from Katherine Symons); *Musical Opinion* (articles on Butterworth by Robert H. Hull); *The Musical Times* (articles by Ernest Newman on 'Concerning "A Shropshire Lad" and other matters', the late Christopher Palmer on C. W. Orr, John Quinlan on 'A. E. Housman and British composers', and John Rippin on Butterworth; letter from Robert Bowden); Oxford University Press (Cyril Bailey's *Hugh Percy Allen*, Michael Kennedy's *Portrait of Elgar* and *The Works of Ralph Vaughan Williams*, Ralph Vaughan Williams' *National Music and other Essays*, Ursula Vaughan Williams' *R.V.W.* and *Heirs and Rebels*, and Ernest Walker's *A History of Music in England*); Penguin Books Ltd (*British Music of our Time*, edited by A. L. Bacharach); Radley College (issues of *The Radleian* and A. K. Boyd's *The History of Radley College*); Routledge and Kegan Paul (R. P. Graves' *A. E. Housman – The Scholar-Poet* and Vic Gammon's article in *History Workshop Journal* on 'Folk-Song Collecting in Sussex and Surrey'); The Royal College of Music (permission to reprint Butterworth's article in *R.C.M. Magazine* on 'Vaughan Williams' *London Symphony*); Stainer and Bell Ltd (Peter Pirie's introductions to two volumes of Butterworth's songs, and music examples from *I fear thy kisses, Requiescat, I will make you brooches, Two English Idylls, Six Songs from A Shropshire Lad, Bredon Hill and Other Songs, We get up in the morn, In the Highlands*, and *The Banks of Green Willow*); Thames Publishing (*Love Blows as the Wind Blows*); Toccata Press (*Boult on Music*, edited by Martin Anderson, and Geoffrey Self's *The Music of E. J. Moeran*); and White Crescent Press Ltd (J. Wright's article in *The Bedfordshire Magazine* on W. E. Henley).

I am deeply indebted to Margaret Aherne-Hardwidge for her most valuable help with all the photographic material, and also to her sister, Rose Aherne. Sources and permissions are acknowledged in the captions.

Finally, I would like to express my sincere thanks to Martin Anderson for his interest and encouragement, to Tricia Cornish, who has been a most efficient typist, to Guy Rickards for help with the proof-reading, and again to Margaret Aherne-Hardwidge not only for her constant help and enthusiasm but also for her word-processing skills, deployed in preparing the final version of this book.

I

EARLY LIFE

The Butterworth family tree[1] gives some indication of their pedigree since the late eighteenth century, although the family can be traced back to Anglo-Saxon times, a Colonel Francis Butterworth describing it as 'the oldest English clan'.[2] One early family home was Butterworth Hall, built in the mid-twelfth century in the hamlet of Butterworth, Rochdale, Lancashire. This area of rolling hills and bleak moorland may indicate the origin of the name Butterworth (butte = French for 'knoll' or 'isolated hill'; worth = 'homestead' or 'farm'), although 'Butter-farm' has been suggested as a more likely meaning.[3]

Many early documents, usually involving land transactions, refer to various members of the family. The year 1274 was significant: it was when Geoffrey de Butterworth married Alison de Belfield, and moved into Belfield Hall, where the Butterworth family lived in style for over 450 years, although some members of the family continued to live at Butterworth

---

[1] *Cf.* p. 18. I am indebted to the valuable help given here by Susan Murray, daughter of a cousin of George Butterworth, and Colin Butterworth, a distant relative.

[2] Quoted in L. M. Angus-Butterworth, *Some Old Lancashire Halls*, Transactions of the Ancient Monuments Society, Vol. 26, 1982, p. 194, an article which gives details of the Butterworth family history. The author, a distant relative of the composer, is a descendant, on his mother's side, of a former Earl of Angus.

[3] P. H. Reaney, *The Origin of English Place-Names*, Routledge and Kegan Paul, London, 1960, p. 129.

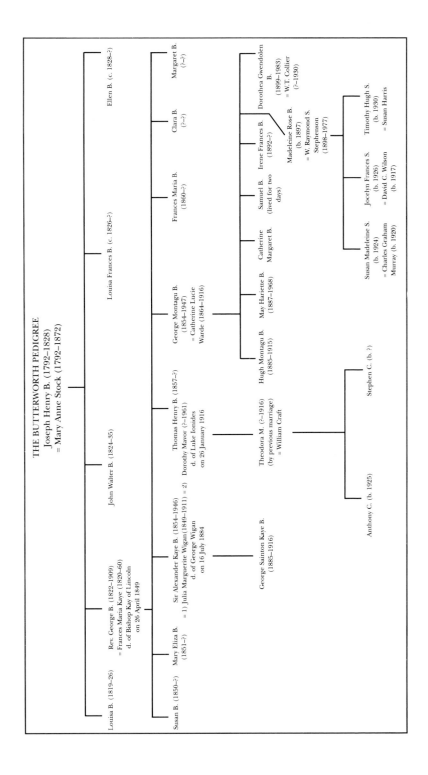

THE BUTTERWORTH PEDIGREE
Joseph Henry B. (1792–1828)
= Mary Anne Stock (1792–1872)

Louisa B. (1819–26)

John Walter B. (1824–35)

Louisa Frances B. (c. 1826–?)

Ellen B. (c. 1828–?)

Rev. George B. (1822–1909)
= Frances Maria Kaye (1820–60)
d. of Bishop Kay of Lincoln
on 26 April 1849

Mary Eliza B.
(1851–?)

Susan B. (1850–?)

Sir Alexander Kaye B. (1854–1946)
= 1) Julia Marguerite Wigan(1849–1911) = 2)
d. of George Wigan
on 16 July 1884

Thomas Henry B. (1857–?)
Dorothy Mavor (?–1961)
d. of Luke Ionides
on 26 January 1916

George Montagu B.
(1854–1947)
= Catherine Lucie
Warde (1864–1916)

Frances Maria B.
(1860–?)

Clara B.
(?–?)

Margaret B.
(?–?)

George Sainton Kaye B.
(1885–1916)

Theodora M. (?–1916)
(by previous marriage)
= William Craft

Hugh Montagu B.
(1885–1915)

May Hariette B.
(1887–1968)

Catherine
Margaret B.

Samuel B.
(lived for two
days)

Irene Frances B.
(1892–?)
Madeleine Rose B.
(b. 1897)
= W. Raymond S.
Stephenson
(1898–1977)

Dorothea Gwendolen
B.
(1899–1983)
= W.T. Collier
(?–1930)

Anthony C. (b. 1925)

Stephen C. (b. ?)

Susan Madeleine S.
(b. 1924)
= Charles Graham
Murray (b. 1920)

Jocelyn Frances S.
(b. 1926)
= David C. Wilson
(b. 1917)

Timothy Hugh S.
(b. 1930)
= Susan Harris

Hall. The last Butterworth to live at Belfield Hall was Alexander Butterworth (1640–1728), High Sheriff of Lancashire, who, at the end of his life, had to hand over the Hall and estates to his steward, Richard Townley.[4] Both halls suffered from gradual decay and were demolished this century, Belfield in 1914, Butterworth in the 1960s.

Joseph Henry Butterworth, son of the Joseph Butterworth who started the Butterworth publishing house, was the composer's great-grandfather. He had five children, one of whom was the Rev. George Butterworth, vicar of Deerhurst, near Tewkesbury, from 1856 to 1893; here was one of the finest Saxon churches in England, equalled only by that at Brixworth, in Northamptonshire, and nearby he discovered another Saxon building, Odda's Chapel.[5] His wife was the younger daughter of Dr John Kaye, Bishop of Lincoln from 1827 to 1853, and her maiden name was given to both Sir Alexander (George Butterworth's father) and the composer himself. In the church are memorial tablets to the Rev. George Butterworth's wife and parents and also a west door, commissioned by Sir Alexander in memory of his son and of his nephew, Hugh Montagu Butterworth, both killed in action during World War I.

Sir Alexander Kaye Butterworth (1854–1946) was one of eight children.[6] Educated at Marlborough and London University, he was called to the Bar at the Inner Temple in 1878 where he practised for five years, before joining the Solicitor's department of the Great Western Railway. There followed a distinguished career as solicitor (1891) to, and General Manager (1906) of, the North Eastern Railway, Sir

[4] Details of both halls can be found in Henry Fishwick, *The History of the Parish of Rochdale*, 1889, pp. 337–46.

[5] For a detailed account of these buildings, *cf.* Edward Gilbert, *A Guide to the Priory Church and Saxon Chapel, Deerhurst, Gloucestershire*, H. Sutherland, Tewkesbury, 1956. The chapel was discovered in 1885, the year of George Butterworth's birth.

[6] The name Alexander had been used in almost every generation since the fourteenth century.

Deerhurst Church and the Butterworth Memorial
(courtesy of M. V. Richardson)

Alexander retiring in 1921. He received a knighthood in 1914 and, from 1923 to 1945, was a director of the new Welwyn Garden City. He was a successful man, with a wide interest in music and the arts, and held the office of chairman of several diverse organisations, both before and after his retirement.

Sir Alexander married twice. His first wife, Julia Marguerite Wigan (1849–1911), was the eldest of nine children of Dr George Wigan, whose great-grandfather had moved to Portishead, near Bristol, around 1750. Before her marriage Julia Wigan was a professional singer and, by all accounts, possessed a fine soprano voice, which may have been one reason for her son's predilection for song.[7] She died on 20 January 1911, and Sir Alexander re-married five years later; his second wife, Dorothea Mavor, daughter of Luke Ionides, the art critic and collector, bore him no children, although she had a daughter, Theodora, by a previous marriage. Their last years were spent at Compton Leigh, a house in Frognal Gardens, Hampstead, where Sir Alexander died at the age of 92, outliving his son by 30 years.

George Sainton Kaye[8] Butterworth, the only child of Alexander and Julia, was born on 12 July 1885 at 16 Westbourne Square, Paddington, London. The family moved to York in 1891 (living at 'Riseholme',[9] 3 Driffield Terrace, The Mount), when Sir Alexander began his career as solicitor to

---

[7] Her 'beautiful singing' of 'Saper vorreste' from Verdi's *Un Ballo in Maschera* was recalled by Edward Dent, in a letter to Sir Alexander, shortly after George's death (*Scrapbook*, f. 63) and, as early as 1871, critics spoke very highly of her vocal accomplishments. She also composed four songs for high voice, which were published posthumously by Augener in 1913.

[8] George was his grandfather's name, Sainton the name of his mother's singing teacher (Mme Sainton-Dolby, wife of the French violinist and composer Prosper Sainton), and Kaye his grandmother's maiden name. Prosper Sainton (1813–90), grandfather of the composer Philip Sainton (1891–1967), was a close friend of Mendelssohn, Wagner, Liszt and Dickens.

[9] Riseholme is a village, north of Lincoln, where Butterworth's paternal grandmother is buried.

the North Eastern Railway, and remained there until 1910, although from 1896 George spent only his vacations in that city, as he was away at boarding schools and university.

At a very early age, it was clearly evident that the boy possessed not only considerable musical ability but also was far more intelligent than his coevals.[10] Having a talented musician for a mother very likely accounted for his musical gifts, at least in part, and even before he went to his preparatory school he showed signs of a rather unusual talent. As a very small boy, he was able to play a piece called *Rousseau's Dream* in twelve keys.[11] His father had, the previous day, promised him five shillings as soon as he could achieve this feat; the young Butterworth, with the modesty characteristic of his later years, thought this reward far too much for so simple a task.

In the summer of 1896, Butterworth was sent to Aysgarth Preparatory School in North Yorkshire, shortly after the school had moved into its present buildings near Bedale. Here he was to spend ten terms, until July 1899, before moving to Eton. He seems to have made a considerable impression, both personally and musically, his musical ability being displayed in organ-playing and composition. The school chapel had a fine three-manual organ which he enjoyed playing, and occasionally he sent home small hymn-tunes, composed without the aid of an instrument.[12] During school vacations, he continued his musical studies in York, with Christian G. Padel, a teacher to whom he owed much, and of whom he always spoke respectfully. Padel (1845–1930) was a prominent figure in the musical life of York, and a pianist and teacher for more than 50 years in that city alone.

---

[10] A friend in York, Anne Middleton, remembered him as a 'little boy, independent and thoughtful beyond his age' (*Scrapbook*, f. 93).

[11] *Rousseau's Dream* is a tune derived from *Le Devin du Village*, an opera by Jean-Jacques Rousseau (1752). The title was apparently given by Johann Baptist Cramer (1771–1858), pianist, composer and founder of the music-publishing firm, and the tune is to be found in some hymn collections.

[12] Three of these hymn-tunes survive (*Scrapbook*, ff. 548–50).

Butterworth as a child (from the Butterworth Memorial Volume)

A pupil of Moscheles in Leipzig, he apparently excelled in the music of Chopin, Beethoven and Liszt.

Butterworth's academic progress was promising, but it was doubtless his qualities of leadership, which reached fruition during his military career in the early years of World War I, that made him stand out among his fellows, and led to his appointment as school captain for the final two terms. Soon after his death, a master at Aysgarth wrote of his vivid re-collection of the boy:

> He came to school rather late, obviously accustomed to the society of older people and unversed in school fashions. But he was a clever lad and soon made his way among his fellows, and latterly took the lead and was much looked up to by younger boys. His undoubted popularity was largely based on his kindness and willing helpfulness to newcomers and those who might for any reason be at a disadvantage.[13]

---

[13] *Memorial Volume*, pp. 5–6; the author's name is unrecorded.

Butterworth as a child (from the Butterworth Memorial Volume)

No doubt his skill in music and games (especially cricket) contributed still more to his popularity. The same master tells how, on entering for the Eton Scholarship, Butterworth was

> so anxious to gain his object, and so keen to conceal his anxiety. In short he stands out in my recollection as one of the remarkable characters in a long list and I felt sure that he would make his mark in whatever career he decided upon.[14]

In 1899, Butterworth gained fourth place in the Eton Foundation Scholarship results and thereby admission to Eton College. Here he led an active life in music and games, although his academic record was not exceptional. He gained quite an impressive list of sports prizes, and held important positions during his five years at the school. He was

---

[14] *Ibid.*, p. 6.

Aysgarth Preparatory School (courtesy of Aysgarth Preparatory School)

clearly an all-round athlete, even from his first year, and was equally distinguished in various musical fields, although, perhaps surprisingly, he appeared in only five concerts, primarily as a pianist. His playing apparently showed sensitivity, and other strong musical attributes included a first-rate sight-reading ability and the gift of absolute pitch.

The *Eton College Chronicles* mention the following occasions when Butterworth participated in school concerts: on 5 June 1900, playing Chopin's *Nocturne* in E flat; on 7 February 1901, the Intermezzo and Scherzino from Schumann's *Faschings-schwank aus Wien*; on 28 March 1901, he played a duet (Edward German's *Humoresque*) with H. M. Knatchbull-Hugesen, which was described as being 'neatly played [but] scarcely appreciated as much as it deserved to be'. On 28 June 1901, he played in two items for two pianos, eight hands (one of Schubert's *Marches Militaires*, D733, and the 'Brautlied' from Wagner's *Lohengrin*), and on 2 April 1903 he performed the Rondo from Mozart's G minor Piano Quartet, 'which the audience hardly appreciated'. More importantly, Butterworth also conducted his own *Barcarolle* for orchestra in this programme, which was, apparently, well played. The composer's appearance was 'a signal for a torrent of applause', which was again continued after the performance.

Butterworth began composing seriously during his time at Eton, studying with Charles Harford Lloyd, the Precentor (i.e., the Director of Music), and Thomas Dunhill, Lloyd's assistant.[15] Although Dunhill taught Butterworth the piano, there is no doubt that he was also an important influence and inspiration behind the early compositions. In a letter to Sir Alexander in September 1916, Dunhill wrote:

> he did his earliest compositions under my guidance – a violin sonata and a little orchestral piece [presumably the *Barcarolle*], besides a great deal of counterpoint. [. . .] He was one of the best pupils I ever had.[16]

Butterworth frequently referred with gratitude to the help he had received from his teacher, whose diaries nonetheless make no mention of him. Neither the violin sonata, the *Barcarolle*, nor a string quartet,[17] all dating from his time at Eton, exist today. They were probably destroyed by the composer before he went to France in 1915. Nothing seems to be known about the first and third works, but the orchestral piece, Butterworth's first 'serious composition',[18] began life in the form of sketches made during a holiday in Scotland with his parents. Throughout his time at Eton, and later, he carried with him musical sketchbooks, in which ideas were jotted down from time to time.

[15] Lloyd (1849–1919) was previously organist of Gloucester Cathedral and Christ Church, Oxford, and a composer of songs, and church and other choral music. Dunhill (1877–1946) was noted as a composer of piano, orchestral and chamber music, of songs (*The Cloths of Heaven*, for example) and, in particular, an operetta, *Tantivy Towers*. He taught at Eton from 1899 to 1908.

[16] *Scrapbook*, f. 41.

[17] The early quartet is mentioned in *Eton College Chronicle*, 19 December 1916, but nowhere else.

[18] *Memorial Volume*, p. 8.

In the autumn of 1904, Butterworth entered Trinity College, Oxford, to read Greats (a BA in Classics), his father wishing him to follow a legal career. But musical activities increased during his four years there, much to the consternation of his college tutor, and resulted in poor academic results (Class III in his Finals in 1908, although he obtained a Class II in Moderations (BA Part I) two years earlier). Everyone who knew him realised that his degree was no reflection of his real ability, but simply the result of spending too much time on music, whether composing, performing, organising concerts, collecting and arranging folksongs, or taking an active part in the University Musical Club. According to his cousin, Madeleine Stephenson,[19] he could think of nothing but music. While still at Oxford, he decided on a career in music, much to his father's disapproval; but Sir Alexander soon gave way and, after George's death, regretted his earlier opposition to his son's inclinations towards music.

On going up to Oxford, Butterworth took with him the score of a recently completed work for small orchestra (presumably the *Barcarolle*), and quickly became engrossed in musical activities with his fellow students. His influence on Oxford music was strong for an undergraduate, and it came as no surprise when he was elected President of the University Musical Club. Hugh Allen, then organist of New College, and a leading figure in Oxford's musical life, wrote of Butterworth's standing as President of the Club:

> he established a reputation for directness of method and brevity of speech. His programmes were unquestionable and progressive, and his rulings in business were autocratic but wholesome [...]. Fearless in debate, a hater of cant, he said many things hard to be borne. Yet he never made an enemy [...] .[20]

---

[19] Letter from Susan Murray, Madeleine Stephenson's daughter, to Robert Gower, November 1987.

[20] 'George Butterworth and his Work', *The Times Literary Supplement*, 26 April 1917 (*Scrapbook*, ff. 132–33).

During his time at Oxford, it was natural for Butterworth to come into contact with other musicians, some of them already important figures in British musical life. Three men were very close friends at this time and, indeed, until his death: Allen, Vaughan Williams and Cecil Sharp, although there is no doubt that his friendship with other musicians, such as Cyril Rootham, R. O. Morris,[21] and many more, had considerable influence on his musical development during the Oxford years.

Allen was of considerable help to Butterworth, whom he thought very promising, and he wrote to Sir Alexander after the composer's death saying that, of all the Oxford under-graduate musicians he had known, his son stood out as 'the most original, the most impatient of humbug [and] the most gifted in the real meaning of things'.[22] Even after he had left Oxford, Butterworth was a regular visitor to Allen's house, and there frequently met Adrian Boult,[23] whose Oxford career began in 1908, and other musicians, among them Reginald Lennard, Francis Jekyll and Bevis Ellis. Butterworth also accompanied Allen on some of his legendary yachting voyages, together with Ellis, Jekyll, Morris and others.

Butterworth's interest in folk music began around 1906, thus marking something of a turning-point in his musical

[21] Rootham (1875–1938) was a Cambridge musician, who ultimately became organist of St John's College; and Morris (1886–1948) was a notable teacher and writer of theoretical works, although his reputation as a composer has largely been forgotten.

[22] *Scrapbook*, f. 46.

[23] They first met at Reading on 1 March 1910, at a concert conducted by Allen. Boult sang the bass solo in Bach's *Magnificat*, and Butterworth played the two-piano accompaniment with Henry Ley (then organist of Christ Church, Oxford) of Stanford's *Ave atque Vale*. When Boult took over the presidency of the Oxford University Musical Club the following year, he asked Butterworth to be the pianist in his first concert (24 January 1911), which included piano trios by Beethoven ('Archduke') and Brahms (Op. 8), but Butterworth apparently withdrew two days before the concert.

Alexander Kaye Butterworth in 1906 (courtesy of The Mansell Collection)

development.[24] The similar interests, and consequent friendship, of Vaughan Williams and Sharp were of paramount
importance in the formation of his musical style from this
time onwards. In 1906, he became a member of the Folk
Song Society, and within a short time proved himself to be a
conscientious and fastidious collector and arranger of folk
tunes.

  Allen wrote[25] that there was no better influence for him
than that of Vaughan Williams,

---

[24] *Cf.* chapter IV, pp. 71–97.

[25] *Loc. cit.*, f. 133.

Sir Hugh Allen (courtesy of the Royal College of Music)

and no friendship more stimulating. The high value that each set upon the other's opinion, and the independence of view which each maintained and cherished, did more than anything else to bring out the latent power of [Butterworth], and set him on the road to great achievement in composition.

Had Butterworth not come into contact with Sharp and Vaughan Williams, had he not been introduced to folk music at this time, and had his musical training been more formal, one may well assume that his achievements would have been far less significant. Butterworth and Vaughan Williams, indeed, were sincere admirers of each other's work.[26]

Apart from his organisational abilities, arranging of concerts and immersion into folk music, Butterworth was not idle in practical music-making, and took part in at least one

[26] *Cf.* pp. 119–124.

concert in the Oxfordshire village of Lower Heyford, accompanying Ferdinand Speyer,[27] a violinist from Balliol College, in sonatas by Beethoven, Mozart and Brahms. At this concert, Butterworth first met Reginald Lennard, who became another close friend. Lennard organised several other concerts in and around Lower Heyford; he was the son of the village rector, and later became Sub-Warden of Wadham College and an eminent historian. Sir Adrian Boult told of the usual procedures at these concerts:[28] train from Oxford to Lower Heyford, a 'sumptuous' tea at the rectory, 'interspersed with frantic rehearsing' before the concerts, some of which took place in the nearby village of Steeple Aston. Butterworth would also have become acquainted with many musicians through performances at Gunfield, an Oxford house where much enjoyable and informal music-making took place.[29]

An Oxford anecdote about Butterworth and R. O. Morris is of some interest.[30] In about 1906, Hugh Allen remarked to Reginald Lennard on seeing the two young men approaching Blackwell's bookshop: 'there goes more red revolution than in the whole of Russia', by which he meant that hostile reaction to the British musical establishment, then quite prevalent. The 'non-academic' Elgar and Delius were establishing themselves, as were such individualists as Holst, Bax, Brian and many more; Vaughan Williams and Butterworth were immersed in folk music, and some of the most 'anti-establishment' composers formed the so-called Frankfurt Group (Scott, Balfour Gardiner, Grainger, O'Neill and Quilter).

---

[27] They had performed together at Eton a few years earlier.

[28] *My Own Trumpet*, Hamish Hamilton, London, 1973, pp. 29–30.

[29] For further details on Gunfield, *cf.* Sir Thomas Armstrong, 'Gunfield Remembered', *Oxford*, Vol. XXVIII, No. 1, May 1976, pp. 78–82.

[30] Information from Sir Thomas Armstrong (in a letter to the author, dated 23 May 1979), to whom it was related by Lennard. It also appears in the introduction (by Sir Thomas) to the miniature score of *A Shropshire Lad* Rhapsody (Eulenburg, London, 1981).

On leaving Oxford in 1908, Butterworth's main concern was making a living, and for the next two years, before he entered the Royal College of Music, he was occupied in musical criticism and teaching. To live by composition alone was out of the question, and so for a time he became assistant music critic for *The Times*, along with H. C. Colles, both of them working under J. A. Fuller Maitland, the chief critic.[31] Little is known of Butterworth during 1908–9, when he lived at 10 Torrington Square, adjacent to London University. He apparently showed in his criticism a 'surprising breadth of certainty of judgment for so young a man, and a most unfaltering denunciation of anything false or meretricious'.[32] In spite of good reports, he was perfectly content to leave behind what he considered an uncongenial way of life, although Colles, after succeeding Fuller Maitland in 1911, did occasionally ask him to submit some critical writing for *The Times*.

The years 1909 to 1910 were spent teaching at Radley College. In spite of the shortness of his stay, Butterworth proved a popular figure in school music and on the games field. One of his musical tasks was to take charge of the piano teaching. Music at Radley was then at quite a low ebb, with no music society, although before the turn of the century an Orpheus Society had lasted for only a few years.

Among Butterworth's main achievements at the school was the formation of a Choral Society, early in 1910, which, as a contemporary account remarks, was hoped to supply 'a long-felt want, and prove a source of strength to the choir'. It

---

[31] Colles worked for *The Times* for 38 years, until his death in 1943, and edited the third and fourth editions of *Grove's Dictionary of Music and Musicians* (Macmillan, London, 1927 and 1940). When Fuller Maitland left *The Times* in 1911, he had already become a pioneer in the folk song revival, publishing, with Lucy Broadwood, *English County Songs* (Cramer, 1893). He also edited the second edition of *Grove's Dictionary* (1904–10) and was a noted champion of Stanford.

[32] *Memorial Volume*, p. 10.

*Ralph Vaughan Williams around 1910
(courtesy of Ursula Vaughan Williams)*

continues: 'Mr. Butterworth is almost entirely responsible for its beginning, and we hope that the Society will flourish as it deserves. [. . .] We hope that in time this Society may extend its influence beyond the vocal sphere and raise an instrumental band'.[33] He rehearsed the Society in Stanford's *The Revenge*, but it is not known if a performance took place.

There seems to be little evidence of Butterworth's taking part in Radley concerts, although in his first term he participated in a chamber recital, in which 'his delightful rendering of the piano part induces us to look forward to the enjoyment in the future of many good things from his store and skill'.[34] No mention of him appears in reports of other musical events, but it seems that 'Mr. Butterworth kindly consented to play through Grieg's music to the play [*Peer Gynt*] in his rooms',[35] to the Senior Intellectual Society, whose members were studying Ibsen's work.

A colleague on the staff at Radley wrote of his impressions of the composer,[36] and the qualities of his character are admirably summed up in phrases which were to become much associated with him: he had 'extraordinary strength of character', he was 'intolerant of narrow-mindedness and inefficiency', he possessed 'a rugged directness of manner', and so on. Butterworth had little opportunity of knowing the majority of the boys, or of being known by them, but he was apparently regarded as an enthusiastic games player, especially of fives, racquets and cricket. The same master described him as being 'too big a man to live happily in small surroundings. The cloistered aloofness of school life bored

---

[33]   *The Radleian*, 19 February 1910.

[34]   *The Radleian*, 27 November 1909. The recital, which took place three weeks earlier, included Beethoven's 'Ghost' Trio, movements from Schubert's Trio in B flat, as well as vocal and violin solos. Butterworth was the pianist in all the items.

[35]   *The Radleian*, 26 March 1910.

[36]   *Memorial Volume*, p. 11; the author's name is unknown.

R. O. Morris, around 1928 (courtesy of the Royal College of Music)

him, and its ecclesiasticism jarred'.[37] It has been pointed out[38] that Radley's musical climate was not congenial to such a distinguished musician, and Butterworth himself wished to leave and improve his technique, which he considered inadequate.

Very little is known of any composing Butterworth may have undertaken while at Radley. His earliest surviving song, *I fear thy kisses,*[39] belongs to 1909, and there is a reference by Boyd to *A Shropshire Lad* Rhapsody having been composed there;[40] but this seems most unlikely, as the song *Loveliest of*

[37] *Ibid.*

[38] A. K. Boyd, *The History of Radley College, 1847–1947*, Blackwell, Oxford, 1948, p. 267.

[39] *Cf.* p. 40.

[40] *Ibid.*

The Lodge, Radley College (courtesy of M. V. Richardson)

trees, upon which the orchestral piece is partly based, bears the dates 'Dec. 31, 1910–Jan. 1, 1911', over one bar in the original score. It is much more likely that the *Shropshire Lad* songs began life here, as the original manuscript is dated '1909/1911'.[41]

Before he left Radley, Butterworth returned to Eton to take part in a concert of compositions by Old Etonians. In this concert, on 26 June 1910, he and E. R. Speyer (possibly a relation of Ferdinand) gave the premiere of Butterworth's *Duo for Two Pianofortes: Rhapsody on English Folk Tunes*, the score of which has been lost (or was destroyed by the composer). He also partnered Frederick Kelly in the last movement of Parry's *Grosses Duo* for two pianos. Other performers at this concert included Roger Quilter accompanying his own songs, sung by Christopher Stone, and, as the final item, Parry himself conducting *Rule, Britannia*.

---

[41] A full discussion of these songs appears in chapter III, pp. 55–65.

In 1910 Butterworth's parents moved from York to London, to live at 19 Cheyne Gardens, Chelsea, very close to Vaughan Williams; this address remained Butterworth's home until 1914.

Butterworth entered the Royal College of Music in 1910, at the age of 25, because he felt the insufficiency of his technique, just as Vaughan Williams, in 1908 and at 36, had gone to Ravel in Paris. Butterworth 'had been advised [...] to undertake work involving more thorough technical knowledge than he possessed, both of piano and organ playing', and he could have thought himself 'musically too much of an amateur'.[42] He remained a student from October 1910 to November 1911,[43] abandoning the course because of his dissatisfaction with the quality of the music he was studying and playing. His first study was organ (with Sir Walter Parratt) and his second piano (with Herbert Sharpe), while harmony, counterpoint and composition were taught by Charles Wood, who thought very highly of him – as did Parry, then Director of the RCM.[44]

Since leaving Oxford, then, Butterworth had gained little satisfaction, as a critic, as a schoolmaster and as a student. Composition appeared to be one way in which to occupy himself, but, even here, there were difficulties: he lacked the necessary fluency in his creative work that some of his contemporaries possessed, although his technical facility was never in doubt, and, in general, the process of composition

---

[42] *Memorial Volume*, p. 12.

[43] College records give these dates, although, surprisingly, all other references state that he spent *less* than a year there.

[44] Parry's name is not often linked with Butterworth's, but one interesting point is worth noting. In 1916, Robert Bridges suggested that Parry should set Blake's *Jerusalem* as a song for massed voices, and that if Parry felt unable to write it, the task should go to Butterworth (*cf.* C. L. Graves, *Hubert Parry: His Life and Works*, London, 1926, Vol. 2, p. 92; quoted in Stephen Banfield, *Sensibility and English Song*, Cambridge University Press, Cambridge, 1985, Vol. 1, p. 137).

19 Cheyne Gardens (courtesy of M. V. Richardson)

kept him busy for a while, perhaps a month or two, only to be followed by a barren period. He thus became a little dissatisfied with life, although it seems his sense of humour always pulled him through.

II

EARLY WORKS

Butterworth's creative output can be divided into four groups: 'early' works, the Housman settings, the folksong revival, and 'late' works.[1] In a creative life barely spanning a dozen years (or a mere five where surviving compositions are concerned), the epithets 'early' and 'late' require some explanation. Butterworth's 'late' works, three orchestral works and a song-cycle, form a group dating from 1911 to 1914. The 'early' works include five from the years 1909–11: three songs, the *Suite* for string quartet and the *Two English Idylls* for small orchestra.

Butterworth was extremely self-critical as a composer, and it is known that, before going off to war in 1914, he destroyed a considerable number of songs, most of them, one presumes, early in date, although no details are known. There is evidence of seven other works which have not survived, including the three compositions from his Eton days (*Barcarolle*, a violin sonata and a string quartet) and the *Duo for Two Pianos*. There is also *Firle Beacon*, a 'beautiful little piano piece', according to Vaughan Williams,[2] and two songs sent to Butterworth's father by a friend: *Crown winter with green* and *Haste on, my joys!*, both to words by Robert Bridges. Sir Alexander described them as 'slight in character, and evidently early in date'.[3]

---

[1] Discussed in chapter V, pp. 98–117.

[2] *Memorial Volume*, p. 92. Firle Beacon is a noted viewpoint on the Sussex Downs, behind Newhaven and Seaford.

[3] *Ibid.*, p. 109.

Early Songs

One of Butterworth's earliest surviving works is his 1909
setting of Shelley's brief poem, *I fear thy kisses*. There are
glimpses here of the composer's characteristically imaginative and delicate style, with a sensitive accompaniment,
foreshadowing in places some of the Housman songs of a
year or so later. The recurring introductory figure, indeed, is
referred to in 'On the idle hill of summer', from the *Bredon
Hill* cycle (Ex. 1).[4]

Ex. 1

(a)   *I fear thy kisses*

(b)   'On the idle hill of summer'

Butterworth's piano accompaniments are, almost without
exception, deftly written and with not a note too many, and
this early example prepares the way for more accomplished
songs from his pen, although one commentator remarked on
its lack of finish, 'Butterworth probably not having ceased
working upon it'.[5] Certainly the piano interlude between the
two verses is a little weak; but that apart, it is a fine song.[6]

---

[4] *Cf.* p. 69.

[5] Stanley A. Bayliss, 'George Butterworth, An Appreciation', *Musical
Mirror*, August 1930, p. 228.

[6] Bax, William Hurlstone and John Gerrard Williams all wrote early
settings of *I fear thy kisses*, in 1906, 1897 and 1913 respectively.

Requiescat, an epitaph for a young girl, belongs to March 1911, two months after the death of Butterworth's mother – a significant fact? Oscar Wilde was perhaps initially a strange choice of author for Butterworth to set, so different were their outlooks, but as Peter Pirie points out, 'Wilde was capable of short lyrics of extraordinary innocence'.[7] The outcome is a song of real beauty, the gentle pathos of Wilde's lines being perfectly matched by the music, whose melodic shapes are characteristic of Butterworth, with, at one point, an almost Finzi-like example of word-setting (Ex. 2).

Ex. 2

The F minor tonality modulates briefly at the climactic point, 'I vex my heart alone, She is at rest', to sharp keys far removed from the original (Ex. 3).

Ex. 3

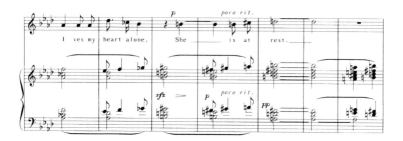

As always, the accompaniment is delicate and deceptively straightforward. There are no weak moments in this song,

---

[7] Introduction to *Folk Songs from Sussex and Other Songs by George Butterworth*, Stainer and Bell, London, 1974, p. iii.

although Ernest Walker believed Butterworth's touch to be 'much less sure when he tried to deal with more sophisticated ideas', citing this example;[8] and Robert H. Hull goes as far as saying that *Requiescat* was the 'only [...] instance in which Butterworth may have mistaken his powers. He is not quite at ease'.[9]

Butterworth's setting of R. L. Stevenson's *I Will Make You Brooches* bears no date and, as with the two previous songs, it was published posthumously. This setting does seem to be one of its composer's less convincing songs, perhaps for two reasons: first, the words largely suggest a rhythm of their own, resulting in a somewhat monotonous effect on Butterworth's part; and second, it has been overshadowed by Vaughan Williams' slightly earlier and more famous setting in *Songs of Travel*.[10] Monotony – the constant $\frac{6}{8}$ metre apart – could also have been avoided by less repetition of bars or phrases, as at the beginning of verse 1. Here, three of the four short vocal phrases are almost identical, accompanied by a repetitive thick-textured piano part (Ex. 4). Admittedly, matters do improve, and the music naturally builds up to a climactic conclusion.

Suite for String Quartet

None of Butterworth's chamber music has ever been published; indeed, only one work in this genre survives, the *Suite* for string quartet (not to be confused with the early quartet from his Eton days[11]). This suite exists, in the composer's hand, in the Bodleian Library, and, although undated, it was probably written around 1910. Allen[12] claims that it is earlier than the Henley song-cycle, *Love Blows as the Wind Blows*, of

[8] *A History of Music in England*, Oxford University Press, Oxford and London, 1907 (revised 1924, 1951), p. 353.

[9] 'George Butterworth' (Part 2), *Musical Opinion*, January 1933, p. 310.

[10] Here called 'The Roadside Fire', the poem's last three words.

[11] *Cf* note 17, p. 26, above.

[12] *Scrapbook*, f. 134.

Ex. 4

1911/12, while the composer gives his Chelsea address on
the score (the family moved there in 1910). Again, as Robert
Bowden states, 'the score shows a developed style of hand
writing and compares with later MSS'.[13]

The *Suite* contains five movements, in each of which folksong influence is apparent. The first, *Andante con moto*, opens
with a viola theme (Ex. 5) in C minor, strongly reminiscent of
many a folk tune, but here no doubt entirely original.

Ex. 5

This flowing movement in $\frac{6}{8}$ reaches its climax in a section in

[13] Letter to *The Musical Times*, Vol. cvii, No. 1485, October 1966, p. 879, in
response to John Rippin's two-part article in the previous two issues.

A flat minor, before the resumption of earlier material. An extremely brief *Scherzando* in B flat follows, again opening with solo viola (Ex. 6), and includes interesting syncopated effects and complex rhythms.

Ex. 6

The central movement, *Allegro molto*, is in a modal G minor, and, yet again, opens with viola (Ex. 7).

Ex. 7

The brisk $\frac{6}{8}$ metre is contrasted with a middle section in A flat (Ex. 8), before a return of the opening, which builds up to a climax in the major key.

Ex. 8

An expressive slow movement follows, with flattened sevenths again prominent (Ex. 9), while the finale, reverting to C

Ex. 9

minor, is perhaps less successful – there are some rather contrived parts, particularly towards the end. Two basic themes (Exx. 10 and 11) bear the imprint of folksong but, in places, their development shows Butterworth losing inspiration.

Ex. 10

Ex. 11

In general, the work is an interesting one. It has some weak moments but also some fine passages of string-writing, whether in the vigorous cross-rhythms of the *Scherzando* or in the lyrical melodies of the slower movements. Perhaps the *Suite* may one day be published, and one hopes that enterprising quartets will include it in their repertoire.

Two English Idylls
The final work in this 'early' phase of Butterworth's output is his first surviving orchestral piece, *Two English Idylls*. Composed in 1910/11, the *Idylls* received their first performance

on 8 February 1912, in Oxford Town Hall, at a concert of the Oxford University Musical Club; the conductor was Hugh Allen. This performance, alongside music by Mozart, Bach and Brahms, was well received, the second *Idyll* being encored. *The Times* commented that the work revealed 'the highest promise, showing great individuality of harmony and orchestration, and a singularly fresh and subtle imaginativeness'.[14] The composer was no doubt pleased with this cordial reception, although his main feeling 'was one of indignation with a harpist who had [. . .] played her part precisely as he had told her not to play it'.[15]

Although styled for 'small orchestra', Butterworth employs double woodwind (plus piccolo), four horns, percussion, harp and strings. The orchestration is particularly fine and delicate, while the treatment of the basically simple thematic material is of a high quality throughout.

The first *Idyll* makes use of three folk tunes. Problems posed by basing works of this nature on folk material are twofold: the linking of the tunes with relevant material, and the treatment of the tunes themselves. Butterworth's skill in both respects is readily apparent, and one can only disagree with Constant Lambert's famous dictum that 'the whole trouble with a folksong is that once you have played it through, there is nothing much you can do except play it over again and play it rather louder'.[16]

Woodwind are prominent throughout the first *Idyll*. The opening theme, announced by the oboe, is derived from *Dabbling in the dew*, a well-known Sussex folksong, with many variants (Ex. 12).[17]

---

[14] Quoted in the *Memorial Volume*, p. 109.

[15] Reginald Lennard's appreciation in the *Memorial Volume*, p. 100.

[16] *Music Ho! A Study of Music in Decline*, Faber and Faber, London, 1934 (reprinted Penguin Books, Harmondsworth, 1948, p. 117); 3rd edition, 1966, p. 146.

[17] This version is very similar to Francis Jekyll's, rather than Butterworth's own (*cf.* Ex. 29 on p. 81).

Ex. 12

Strings provide a subdued accompaniment. Flute and clarinet take up the theme, followed by oboe again, this time in D
flat, accompanied by busy semiquaver figures in the strings.
Speed and volume are reduced as the oboe introduces the
second folksong, *Just as the tide was flowing*, first collected by
Butterworth in Sussex in April 1907 (Ex. 13 compares the
versions of Butterworth and Vaughan Williams). This tune is
then repeated by flute and by strings.

Ex. 13

(a)   Butterworth

(b)   Vaughan Williams

A livelier section, *Molto vivace*, reveals the third tune,
Henry Martin (first collected by Butterworth in Sussex in
June 1907), played by clarinet (Ex. 14), then by flute and
bassoon.

Ex. 14

After general development, a *fortissimo* version of the second
theme is heard in the strings, in B flat. A climax is reached,
then suddenly all goes quiet, with oboe and flute sharing
equally the opening theme. In the final bars, the busy string
figures recur, and all ends peacefully.

The second *Idyll* uses only one main theme, *Phoebe and her
dark-eyed sailor,* first collected by the composer in Sussex in
April 1907. Compared with its predecessor, this is a slower,
softer and more contemplative piece of writing, beautifully
scored, and again with solo oboe announcing the tune
(Ex. 15), accompanied by two bassoons.

Ex. 15

Flute and first violins take up the theme, with fuller scoring,
leading to a *Molto sostenuto* section, in which clarinet and flute
develop the tune in C minor. Although the main characteristic of this piece is of a gentle lyricism, the music does move
towards a climax of some breadth and power, before a quiet
ending. Towards the close, a solo violin plays a decorated
version of the tune in canon with a solo clarinet.

It is interesting to note that Allen[18] reverses the numbering
of the *Idylls* – were they, indeed, first performed in that order?

[18] *Loc. cit.*, f. 134.

Butterworth's father must have discussed this same point with Sir Henry Wood, as Wood wrote to him: 'I quite agree with you about the order, and shall certainly play No. 2 first, at the next performance I direct of them'.[19]

London first heard the *Idylls* at a Queen's Hall Prom on 31 August 1919, conducted by Wood. The reception was favourable. Two years later, Wood again inserted them in a Prom programme, where, rather curiously, they were labelled as 'first performance', one (unnamed) critic then remarking: 'this was a slip, since they were played [...] at the recent Zurich [International Musical] Festival, though they had not been heard before in England'.[20] Wood also conducted the Rhapsody, *A Shropshire Lad*, at Zurich (5 July 1921). The *Idylls* received a second European performance six months later, on 5 January 1922, when Adrian Boult conducted a programme of English music with the Czech Philharmonic Orchestra, in the Smetana Hall, Prague. Butterworth's work was placed alongside Bliss' *Mêlée Fantasque* and Elgar's Symphony No. 2, and apparently 'struck local musicians as rather primitive, but [...] the audience enjoyed them'.[21] Boult then introduced Butterworth to a Barcelona audience on 26 May 1922, when he conducted the first *Idyll* and Holst's ballet music from *The Perfect Fool*, sharing a programme with Casals. Orchestra and audience 'like it [the *Idyll*] immensely'.[22]

Today, the *Idylls* remain comparatively neglected, Butterworth's other two orchestral works receiving more performances, although three recordings came out during the 1970s, two in the late 1980s and one in 1993.

---

[19] Letter to Sir Alexander, 26 October 1921, *Scrapbook*, f. 494. Sir Alexander had been present at a Prom performance of the *Idylls*, directed by Wood on 30 August.

[20] *Westminster Gazette*, 31 August 1921.

[21] Part of Edward Dent's review in *Nation and Athenaeum*, January 1922; *Scrapbook*, ff. 519–20.

[22] Letter from Sir Adrian Boult to Sir Alexander, 7 June 1922; *Scrapbook*, f. 534.

This early phase of Butterworth's output produced, then, five existing works and a quantity of discarded pieces, such was his degree of self-criticism. Two of the three songs bear hallmarks characteristic of the more famous Housman settings: the perfect match of words and music, the economical piano writing, the melodic line, the overall delicate style. The *Suite* for string quartet, the sole surviving chamber work, is an interesting example of the genre, in spite of its imperfections, and the *Two English Idylls* show an imaginative use of harmony and orchestration which look forward to the Rhapsody, *A Shropshire Lad* and *The Banks of Green Willow*.

During the time of composing these works, Butterworth was very active in the folksong revival, and the immersion in this indigenous music was a considerable help in the forging of his musical style.

III

BUTTERWORTH
AND HOUSMAN

Butterworth's finest achievements in song-writing are to be found in his two song-cycles to poems from Housman's *A Shropshire Lad*: the *Six Songs* and *Bredon Hill and Other Songs*. Much has been written about Housman and music – hardly surprisingly, as his simple, direct verses appealed to many composers, and not only British ones. Although the poems were published in February 1896, the first published musical settings in England (by Arthur Somervell) did not appear until 1904. Thereafter Housman and Walt Whitman were to be the favourite poets set by British composers in the early years of the twentieth century.

Alfred Edward Housman (1859–1936), an almost exact contemporary of Elgar, was a notable classical scholar, successively Professor of Latin at London and Cambridge. He was renowned throughout Europe for his scholarship, but remained an enigmatic character in university circles, being regarded as one of the 'most feared men'[1] at Cambridge. In the discussion of poetry, his name is often linked with that of Thomas Hardy, each in his own way representing Victorian pessimism, although the poetic procedures of each writer differed considerably.

A Shropshire Lad was Housman's first book of poems to be published. He created the central character, Terence Hearsay, a young man from Shropshire, who would come to

---

[1] A recollection by Howells in Christopher Palmer, *Herbert Howells: A Study*, Novello, Borough Green, Sevenoaks, 1978, p. 16.

London and, like Housman himself, live there in exile. The poet's home was, in truth, at Bromsgrove, in Worcestershire, and in his childhood he used to walk in the country and look towards the Shropshire hills, for which he had a special affection. The Housman scholar, Richard Perceval Graves, has remarked that Housman's Shropshire 'is largely an imaginary land; and the real place-names were often used for romantic colouring rather than because Housman had a particular feeling for a real place'.[2] Indeed, the poet once said that he wrote six of these poems before setting foot in the county.

In his collection of 63 brief poems, Housman projects the character of the doomed young countryman who, by turns, is represented as soldier, farmer, criminal and lover. These verses of nostalgic restraint soon gave inspiration to a considerable number of composers, and continued to do so for several decades: H. K. Andrews, Thomas Armstrong, Stanley Bate, Arnold Bax, Lennox Berkeley, Ben Burrows, George Dyson, Balfour Gardiner, Armstrong Gibbs, Ivor Gurney, Michael Head, Herbert Howells, John Ireland, Henry Ley, E. J. Moeran, C. W. Orr,[3] Graham Peel, Humphrey Searle, Arthur Somervell, Ralph Vaughan Williams and, of course, George Butterworth. By 1943 the three most popular lyrics to be set to music were 'Loveliest of trees' (by ten composers), 'When I was one-and-twenty' (eight) and 'Bredon Hill' (seven).

In spite of this considerable attraction to Housman's poems, not everyone approved. Constant Lambert, who adopted something of a rebellious attitude to the folksong revival and its associated ideas, wrote in 1934: 'since the Shropshire lad himself published his last poems some ten

[2] *A. E. Housman – The Scholar-Poet*, Routledge & Kegan Paul, London, 1979/Oxford University Press, Oxford and London, 1981, p. 105; *cf.* also George E. Haynes, 'Housman's Shropshire', *Housman Society Journal*, Vol. 20, 1994, pp. 17–21.

[3] Orr (1893–1976) was setting Housman's verses as late as 1952.

A. E. Housman, aged 35, two years before the publication
of A Shropshire Lad *in 1896*
(courtesy of The Housman Society)

years ago it may without impertinence be suggested that it is high time his musical followers published their last songs'.[4]

Several commentators have remarked on Housman's disinterest in music, although their claims are not entirely true. William White is typical of many:

> Housman had little interest in music, rarely (if ever) attended concerts, even disliked listening to music, especially settings of *A Shropshire Lad*, and only once asked to hear Beethoven's 5th because 'he remembered to have heard it well spoken of'.[5]

---

[4] *Op. cit.*, p. 284.

[5] 'A. E. Housman and Music', *Music & Letters*, Vol. XXIV, No. 4, October 1943, p. 210.

Housman's sister, Katherine Symons, immediately rose to the poet's defence, and it is interesting to note what she revealed about his attitude to music as a child and as a young man:

> in boyhood, music attracted my brother in so marked a degree that it came as a surprise to survivors of his family to read, after his death, reminiscences from latter-day friends which appeared to show in [him] ignorance of music, or even antipathy.[6]

He enjoyed learning the piano initially, although he gave it up 'when he found he had no easy aptitude for it'. He also, apparently, appreciated instrumental music at home, had a pleasant baritone voice, and 'certainly had a great desire that his poems should find musical settings that would catch the popular ear'. In adult life, his musical taste was unashamedly popular, rarely veering from the music hall.

The large number of composers attracted to Housman's verses had no difficulty with the poet when they wished to set them to music, and in 1906 he wrote to Grant Richards, his publisher, 'I always give my consent to all composers, in the hope of becoming immortal somehow'.[7] But there was one stipulation: his verses were not to appear on concert programmes, although he did occasionally relax his rule (for example, in the case of Vaughan Williams' *On Wenlock Edge*, in November 1909). In later years, the relationship between composer and poet was far less amicable, when Housman discovered that Vaughan Williams had omitted two verses from 'Is my team ploughing?' The composer's view was that any poet who had written such lines as

> The goal stands up, the keeper
> Stands up to keep the goal

should be grateful to have them left out, a remark not made directly to Housman, but to a friend of Grant Richards. Housman's response to this comment was: 'I wonder how he would like me to cut two bars out of his music', and his

---

[6] Letter in *Music & Letters*, Vol. XXV, No. 1, January 1944, p. 60.

[7] Quoted in Graves, *op. cit.*, p. 117.

reaction was even more bitter on hearing records of the song-cycle.[8] Thus, from a childhood interest in music, Housman grew to condemn certain settings of his poems, including some of the best, although he never prohibited composers from setting his verses to music.

John Quinlan has aptly summed up why composers were so attracted to Housman's poetry: 'The brevity of the lines, their essential Englishness, their pastoral atmosphere, their rhythm, and their simple spontaneity of feeling were contributing factors'.[9] One can add to these elements the prevalent pessimistic atmosphere in some poetry of the time, not least that of Hardy.

In discussing the numerous settings of Housman's poems, most writers have agreed that few composers have ever matched the simplicity and directness of Butterworth's songs, although strong claims have been made for the highly individual songs of Gurney and Orr.[10] Orr has had a few champions over the years but, even so, his songs remain sadly neglected, and one of the few writers not to single out Butterworth has remarked that

> Orr and Vaughan Williams stand together at the head of all British composers who vied with each other for setting Housman to music, and to many it would appear that Orr has on the whole achieved an even greater measure of success in this field than [...] Vaughan Williams.[11]

---

[8] *Ibid.*

[9] 'A. E. Housman and British Composers', *The Musical Times*, Vol. c, No. 1393, March 1959, pp. 137–38.

[10] Of Orr's 36 songs (not 35, as usually quoted), 24 are Housman settings, more than by any other composer. There is an interesting discussion of Orr's songs in Paul Edwards, 'C. W. Orr', *British Music Society News*, No. 60, December 1993, pp. 258–60 and 277–79.

[11] P. M. H. Edwards, *C. W. Orr, A Short Appreciation*, unpublished, Victoria (British Columbia), Canada, no date, pp. 10–12; quoted in Joseph T. Rawlins, 'Charles Wilfred Orr (1893–1976)', *Composer*, No. 74, Winter 1981, p. 25.

The influence of folksong undoubtedly helped Butterworth to illustrate the essential spirit of Housman's words,
thereby creating a distinctively lyrical form of English song.
His simple, delicate settings fully express the nostalgia and
sentiment found in Housman's verses, and it is this perfect
match of poem and music which has appealed to singers and
listeners alike. Very few of his contemporaries expressed
their musical thoughts in such an economical way. Rutland
Boughton,[12] one of the most enthusiastic early champions of
Butterworth's song-cycles, commented on the 'inevitable'
music allied to the words and on three similar features in the
two men's work: restraint, simplicity, beauty. They also
shared personal characteristics, reserve and self-criticism
being predominant.

Six Songs from 'A Shropshire Lad'

Six Songs from 'A Shropshire Lad' first made Butterworth's
name famous, and the set has since become regarded as a
classic amongst English song-cycles of the twentieth century.
The cycle was completed in 1911, and it received its first
performance and publication in that year. In April 1912
Butterworth donated to Eton College library the autograph
score of all his Housman settings, with the exception of 'On
the idle hill of summer'.[13] Both sets of songs date from the
years 1909 to 1911, although some songs were most likely
conceived in the Oxford years and, in Butterworth's customary manner, each carefully revised until it met with his
complete approval. At first, he intended to group the songs
into one narrative cycle, but later regrouped them into two
sets for publication.

[12] 'Modern British song-writers, IV: George Butterworth', *Music Student*,
December 1913, pp. 85–86.

[13] This is a surprising omission, but it could suggest a slightly later date of
composition. The ten songs come in the following order in the manuscript:
'Oh fair enough', 'Think no more, lad', 'Is my team ploughing?', 'When
the lad for longing sighs', 'Loveliest of trees', 'When I was one-and-twenty',
'The lads in their hundreds', 'With rue my heart is laden', 'Look not in my
eyes' and 'Bredon Hill'.

The first known performance of *Six Songs* took place on 16 May 1911, at a meeting of the Oxford University Musical Club, organised by Adrian Boult; the performers were the baritone J. Campbell McInnes[14] and the composer at the piano. 'The lads in their hundreds' was not performed, although four songs from the *Bredon Hill* cycle were included in the programme (the omission being 'On the idle hill of summer'). The nine songs were not sung in the order known today but as follows: 'Oh fair enough are sky and plain', 'Look not in my eyes', 'When I was one-and-twenty', 'When the lad for longing sighs', 'Think no more, lad', 'Loveliest of trees', 'Is my team ploughing?', 'With rue my heart is laden' and 'In summertime on Bredon'.[15]

The London premiere of *Six Songs* took place on 20 June 1911, at the Aeolian Hall, and was again given by Campbell McInnes, accompanied this time by Hamilton Harty. The work was largely well received, certainly by the audience, who demanded an encore of 'The lads in their hundreds' (then presumably receiving its first performance) and, in most cases, by the critics, although the (unnamed) *Morning Post* reviewer the next day was far from laudatory:

> His studied avoidance of mere melodic attractiveness did not constitute a source of distinction or strength, but rather showed that he had mistrusted his own instincts and substituted effort for inspiration.

'Loveliest of trees'

Of all Housman's poems, this one has probably been set to music more times than any other: at least 35 settings were known in 1976.[16] Butterworth's setting is one of his finest and

---

[14] McInnes (1874–1945) was a noted interpreter of Vaughan Williams' music, and took important solo roles in the premieres of *A Sea Symphony* and *Five Mystical Songs*.

[15] Ten days after the premiere, Boult sang four of the songs at Allen's house, with Allen accompanying (Michael Kennedy, *Adrian Boult*, Hamish Hamilton, 1987, p. 50).

[16] Banfield, *op. cit.*, Vol. 1, p. 242.

one of his best-known, its thematic material forming the basis of the orchestral Rhapsody.[17] The poem tells of a young man of twenty admiring the cherry tree in bloom, while simultaneously regretting the rapid passing of life, even with fifty more years in which to renew his admiration. This is more than a little ironic, as Peter Pirie has remarked:[18] Housman was in his mid-thirties when he wrote the poem, while Butterworth had but five or six years of life left to him.

The opening bars are deceptive in their simplicity, and pose problems for pianist and singer alike. Even Butterworth had difficulty in conveying his exact requirements, changing the original *Andante molto teneramente* to the present *Molto moderato, sempre rubato e con espressione*. The fine melodic contour of the piano introduction, perhaps suggesting the falling cherry blossom, sets a calm, pastoral atmosphere and leads into the poignant vocal line which forms the basis of the Rhapsody (Ex. 16).

Ex. 16

Love--liest of trees, the cherry now is hung with bloom a---long the bough

The singer's very first bar requires extremely careful handling, as he must enter on a soft high E, requiring just a shade of *rubato*. In the first verse, the vocal line is notable for its sheer melodiousness and originality, and here Butterworth uses what is for him the unusually wide range of a minor tenth. The melodic line at 'Wearing white for Eastertide' and the piano interlude between the first two verses will be familiar to admirers of the Rhapsody.[19] The second verse, in

[17] *Cf.* p. 101.

[18] Introduction to *Eleven Songs from 'A Shropshire Lad'*, Stainer and Bell, London, 1974, p. ii.

[19] *Cf.* Ex. 34 on p. 102.

which the young man reflects on the passing of the years, contains a very sparse accompaniment, while flowing arpeggios underline the vocal part of the final stanza, suggesting progressions from Debussy, as in his first *Arabesque* for piano (1888), also in E major. The vocal line, having changed for verse two, now reverts to the main theme, its two strands appearing in reverse order, thus giving the whole song a symmetrical pattern. The piano epilogue develops the main theme in thirds, a characteristic Butterworth touch.[20]

'When I was one-and-twenty'
In this simple song, Butterworth took a traditional tune in the Dorian mode (Ex. 17).

Ex. 17

Words and music blend well and, as in some of his other Housman settings ('Is my team ploughing?', for example), the tender quality of the music 'softens the cultivated pessimism of the poet's words'.[21] This poem has been popular with composers, and Butterworth's setting of the story of the unheeding young man falling in love but despairing a year later, is a sensitive treatment of the words, the repetition of ''tis true' at the conclusion creating the appropriate hint of sadness. Butterworth's intention of marrying simple verses with simple music is clearly evident here, so at the climactic point of the song, 'And I am two-and-twenty, and oh, 'tis true, 'tis true', the musical content remains unaltered, even in the

[20] *Cf.* the opening bars of the Rhapsody.

[21] Bayliss, *loc. cit.*, p. 212.

accompaniment. C. W. Orr thought quite differently in his setting and wrote (quite rightly, I believe):

> simplicity in verse and in music are not quite the same thing; music should bring out the undertones [...] of what the poet has said, and this simplicity may not always be possible or even desirable in musical settings [...].[22]

'Look not in my eyes'

This song follows on in similar vein, although with specific reference to the Narcissus legend. Its folk-like character is apparent throughout, with the inevitable flattened sevenths, while the almost perpetual $\frac{5}{4}$ time avoids making it yet another four-square folk-tune (Ex. 18).

Ex. 18

The accompaniment now has a thicker texture; not only does it play almost continuously, unlike Butterworth's practice in the first two songs, but also in chords, with (at least) four-part harmony.

---

[22] Letter to Joseph T. Rawlins (1971), in Rawlins, *loc. cit.*, p. 25. Orr, not known for his admiration of Butterworth's songs, referred to 'that atrociously feeble folktune [...] for "When I was one-and-twenty"' (in correspondence with Christopher Palmer, October 1973, and quoted in Banfield, *op. cit.*, Vol. 2, p. 399).

These three songs can be grouped together as being lyrical and full of simple charm. The next three songs have a more dramatic nature.

'Think no more, lad'

The original manuscript gives some indication of how far Butterworth made alterations before the final published form was achieved. The second and third verses underwent drastic changes. Lesser variations include a change in pitch (the original key was G minor, not G sharp minor) and the addition of two introductory bars in the published version. The reckless mood of the poem is well captured in the music, and the off-beat chords (second verse) and rapid arpeggios (third verse) make the piano part more complex than it is elsewhere in this cycle (Ex. 19).

Ex. 19

Butterworth repeats the first verse after the second, with an identical vocal line until the climactic 'falling sky', matched by a more virtuosic accompaniment – an impressive ending.

'The lads in their hundreds'

The message here is simple: young men attend the annual Ludlow fair, perhaps for the last time; and again one senses the irony in the relationship between Butterworth's life and the poems he chose to set to music. This setting poses few musical problems, the lilting vocal line, almost inevitably in a continuously compound time, perfectly fitting the words (Ex. 20), with supporting chords in the piano, except in the 'ritornelli' between the verses and in the coda, where there is considerably more movement.

Ex. 20

In the autograph score, two minor alterations are apparent: the original key was F major (not F sharp major) and the tempo was changed from *Vivace ma non troppo, legato e rubato* to *Allegretto, sempre tranquillo e senza rigore*.

It is a strophic song with scarcely any variation in the accompaniment for each verse, though one feels Butterworth could have altered the music in some way for the final line of all, 'The lads that will die in their glory and never be old'.

Ritornelli and coda make considerable use of the ♩♩♩ rhythm, contrasting with the even quavers of the vocal line; Butterworth's setting nonetheless tends a little towards monotony, in view of its strophic form and the rare use of expression marks, which are limited to a couple of accents and a *crescendo/diminuendo*, in addition to *p sempre* at the beginning.[23]

'Is my team ploughing?'

Housman said of this poem: 'I think it may be my best, though it is not the most perfect'. Butterworth could have said of his setting: 'I think it may be my best *and* the most perfect'. There is no doubt that this remarkable song is the gem, not only of the cycle, but of all his songs, and has even been called 'one of the great songs of the world [...] a lied that challenges comparison with [Schubert's] *Der Doppelgänger*'.[24] It is certainly true that coming after what are essentially fine, straightforward vocal settings, this particular song immediately makes its mark by its sheer simplicity and extremely moving quality.

The dialogue between the dead man and his living friend is most aptly portrayed. Housman's eight verses alternate between these two 'characters', and Butterworth is clearly content to treat each verse strophically, the only major difference coming at the very end of the vocal part. For the rest, each of the dead man's questioning verses is very simply set, always *pianissimo*, and supported by long descending secondary chords in the accompaniment (Ex. 21), taken, it seems, straight from Grieg's String Quartet.[25] As in 'Loveliest of trees', the singer has to begin on a very soft high note, an awkward moment for baritones. A complete change marks the replies of the dead man's friend: a slightly lower vocal line, which is quicker and louder than before, and an accompaniment of long common chords (Ex. 22).

The masterstroke in this song is to be found at the very end: 'I cheer a dead man's sweetheart; Never ask me whose', the words belonging to the friend, while the music of the last phrase, now soft and slow, is that of the dead man, a fact

---

[23] For a detailed discussion of this poem, and of settings by Butterworth, Moeran and Somervell, *cf.* Banfield, *op. cit.*, Vol. 2, pp. 402–5.

[24] Pirie, *loc. cit.*, p. iii.

[25] Banfield, *op. cit.*, Vol. 1, p. 147.

Ex. 21

Ex. 22

accentuated by the use of secondary chords in the accompaniment. This final vocal phrase is altered rhythmically and,
for one note, melodically, compared with other stanzas, and
the effect of the dead man's question remaining unanswered
is heightened by the unresolved minor added-sixth chord at
the end (Ex. 23).

Ex. 23

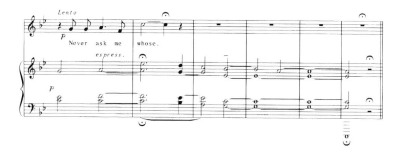

Such simplicity of style in this little masterpiece has not
won universal admiration. Ernest Newman's well-known
castigation of Vaughan Williams' Housman settings, including 'Is my team ploughing?', is somewhat tempered by his
general appreciation of Butterworth's approach to them,
although he felt that 'Butterworth has failed [...] to find the
right musical equivalent for the poignant end of the
poem'.[26]

Christopher Palmer, in championing the songs of C. W.
Orr, readily asserts that Orr's setting is the most successful of
many, as he avoids the 'over-studied simplicity and directness' of Butterworth by a 'skilful interpenetration of diatonic

[26] 'Concerning *A Shropshire Lad* and Other Matters', *The Musical Times*,
Vol. lix, September 1918, pp. 393–98. Newman summed up his tirade
against Vaughan Williams' setting of this poem: 'I cannot imagine any
composer indulging in a greater number of the most egregious artistic
falsities in one song'.

and chromatic elements'.[27] But Butterworth's harmonic and melodic style does not generally run to chromaticism; and that he chooses to write diatonically and with never a superfluous note is scarcely cause for adverse criticism.

In no other song did Butterworth capture so succinctly the mood of the poem, and one can only ponder on what song-settings he might have produced had his life been spared. The *Six Songs* were dedicated to 'V. A. B. K.', that is, Victor Annesley Barrington-Kennett, a contemporary of Butterworth's at Eton (1901–5) and Oxford (1906–10).[28]

In the early 1960s, the *Six Songs from 'A Shropshire Lad'* were orchestrated by Lance Baker, a professional horn-player, a composer, and son of Ruth Gipps. There are no key changes from the published version of the songs, and in his work as a whole Baker has been careful to retain something of the style of the orchestral Rhapsody. Only three performances have been given to date, all by the London Repertoire Orchestra, conducted by Ruth Gipps, and with various soloists.

Bredon Hill

The *Bredon Hill* cycle was published a year after *Six Songs*, in 1912, and seems to have been an immediate success, contemporary writers being full of praise for these charming and original songs with their wealth of melodic and harmonic beauty. Boughton, writing in 1913, believed them to be an advance on their first cycle, and forecast that 'any publication of new songs by George Butterworth will be an event in the musical world'.[29] The piano accompaniments to this cycle are generally more complex, notably in 'On the idle hill of

---

[27] 'C. W. Orr: An 80th birthday tribute', *The Musical Times*, Vol. cxiv, No. 1565, July 1973, p. 691.

[28] His family lived at 19 Cheyne Gardens, Chelsea, the house which the Butterworths purchased in 1910. After graduating in history at Balliol, Victor Barrington-Kennett went to Sandhurst, and later served as a major and a squadron-commander in France. He was killed at Serre on 13 March 1916.

[29] *Loc. cit.*

summer', the finest of the set, and, as a whole, the songs lack the basic simplicity of *Six Songs*, and are less well-known.

'Bredon Hill' ('In summertime on Bredon')

This well-known poem has been set by a number of composers, among them Peel, Somervell and Vaughan Williams, and writers have invariably compared them.[30] The constant reference to bells invites musical imagery in the accompaniment, and whereas some composers have taken this to extremes, Butterworth has been careful not to make his bells too assertive: they are certainly present for much of the time, expressed in flowing quavers, frequently as arpeggios or scalic figures, but they do not dominate the music. Graham Peel's popular setting is essentially strophic, and, with little in the way of descriptive accompaniment, tends towards monotony. A poem of this length, with its seven stanzas, requires variety of musical content, and Butterworth has taken advantage of its dramatic possibilities, although the music really ought to be on a larger scale to do the poem complete justice.

The poem itself briefly describes love, hope and sadness, with constant reference, in words and music, to bells in various circumstances: Sunday, wedding, funeral. This setting is one of Butterworth's most elaborate, and much use is made of recurring ideas (for example, the minute introductory figure (Ex. 24), and the flowing quaver accompaniment).

Ex. 24

---

[30] For example, Brian Blyth Daubney, 'A Range of Hills', *British Music*, Vol. 11, 1989, pp. 7–18, discussing settings by Peel, Somervell, Vaughan Williams, Benjamin Burrows and Butterworth.

Variety is achieved by avoiding a strophic setting, although the first two (sometimes three) lines of each verse are essentially the same; there are also ascending semitonal shifts of key: F to F sharp (end of the second verse), F sharp to G (end of the third verse). Some passionate writing for piano links the fourth and fifth verses, modulating suddenly from A major to G minor; the fifth and sixth verses describe the girl's death and funeral. The headlong rush of quavers in the accompaniment stops abruptly for these two verses, the fifth consisting entirely of long secondary chords, and the sixth introducing the 'one bell only' five times in the bass before descending in step, while the right hand uses the intro-ductory motif. The final stanza, now back in F, contains the climax of the song at 'O noisy bells, be dumb; I hear you, I will come'; here Butterworth uses interesting harmonies, a sudden minor tonality and, very effectively, the whole-tone scale (Ex. 25).

Ex. 25

This is an impressive conclusion to a fine setting. Although the original and final versions of this song are largely the same (there is now one fewer bar in the last verse), Butter-worth completely changed the ending, replacing five bars (Ex. 26) with three rather more static.

'Oh fair enough are sky and plain'
This song appears as the first in the autograph score, and so could well date from 1909. Another 'Narcissus' (self-worship) song, it poses few problems for singer or pianist. The accom-paniment is sparse, largely comprising isolated (or pairs of)

Ex. 26

chords, except in the second verse, where the voice is sub-servient to the piano's rippling of the 'pools and rivers'. The fourth and final verse more or less reverts to the opening music of the song, thus giving some feel of symmetry.

'When the lad for longing sighs'

The folk-like element and gentle lyricism recall 'Look not in my eyes', from the *Six Songs*, and the three short verses produce a song of delicate simplicity. Melody and harmony are straightforward throughout, the piano playing the vocal line of the first verse in the ensuing verses, while the voice merely hints at it (Ex. 27).

Ex. 27

'On the idle hill of summer'

That this setting does not appear in the original manuscript could suggest a slightly later date of composition; and it is the most assured song in the cycle. It is yet another example of the irony in the relationship between Butterworth's life and the choice of poems he set to music. The poet hears soldiers marching in the distance while he idly dreams on a hill but, after meditating on the folly of war, decides to go himself.

Although the accompaniment is the most complex in any
Butterworth song, there are times (in the first and third
verses, and in the closing bars) when it remains static, with
repeated throbbing syncopated added-sixth chords, representing 'the steady drummer drumming like a noise in
dreams', and the chords themselves somehow capturing the
atmosphere of a warm summer's day (Ex. 28).

Ex. 28

The vocal line in the first and third verses (apart from one
note in the latter) is constructed from notes of the added-
sixth chord of A major, but the introduction to the second
verse immediately ushers in a new idea, using dominant
ninths and thirteenths, and builds up to a climax at 'Dear to
friends and food for powder, soldiers marching, all to die'.
The fourth and final verse is considerably more lively, with a
busy piano part (secondary seventh arpeggios to the fore),
portraying 'Bugles' and 'the screaming fife', leading to the
dramatic outburst: 'Woman bore me, I will rise'. During this
verse, the piano has wide stretches in the bass, which, as
Vernon Butcher remarks, is unfortunate, since 'any spread-
ing of the chords will destroy their syncopated nature'.[31] This
somewhat restless rhythm is almost constantly present in the
song.

Some settings of this poem (Somervell's, for instance)
allow the piano to conclude boldly, but Butterworth makes
his accompaniment gradually subside to *pp morendo* in the

---

[31] 'A. E. Housman and the English Composer', *Music & Letters*, Vol. XXIX,
No. 4, October 1948, p. 332.

coda, bringing back the opening drum rhythm, again on repeated added-sixth chords. One can visualise soldiers and drummer gradually retreating – an imaginative ending to this dramatic and very fine song, which is, indeed, one of Butterworth's most assured achievements.[32] Its musical language, far removed from the folksong idiom which here would seem quite out of place, is very much in the mainstream late-Romantic tradition, and the harmonic procedures of such composers as Wagner and Debussy are in evidence.

'With rue my heart is laden'

The simple, elegiac sentiments of the poem most aptly sum up the composer's life, although to Richard Perceval Graves this miniature, like a few other Housman poems, is 'thoroughly inferior'.[33] The folk-like melody is supported throughout by unobtrusive harmonies, and the opening phrase is imaginatively quoted at the end of *A Shropshire Lad* Rhapsody.[34] Words, melody and accompaniment fit each other perfectly, and the song, as a whole, makes a worthy conclusion to the cycle. The 'golden friends' may well have been influenced by Shakespeare's 'Golden lads and girls' (*Cymbeline*, Act IV, Scene 2), a favourite device of Housman's being to rework odd lines of the Bard.

[32] Orr thought this song to be by far Butterworth's finest (Orr in correspondence with Christopher Palmer, October 1973, quoted in Banfield, *op. cit.*, Vol. 2, p. 399).

[33] *Op. cit.*, p. 99.

[34] *Cf.* p. 103.

IV

BUTTERWORTH
AND THE FOLKSONG REVIVAL

After Butterworth left the Royal College of Music in November 1911 – he had not found student life entirely to his satisfaction, and his teaching and music criticism failed to provide the solution – he occupied himself with composition from time to time, without finding in it a cure for his restlessness. The answer lay in total commitment to the folksong revival. Butterworth had, for some years, spent much time collecting and arranging folktunes, since his interest and enthusiasm for them had begun in Oxford and with his first meetings with Vaughan Williams and Cecil Sharp. He joined the Folk Song Society in 1906, eight years after its foundation, and shortly afterwards, in September of that year, began his collecting of folksongs, a task which occupied him intermittently until March 1913. Butterworth was also active with the Oxford Folk Music Society from 1909, and in 1910 he invited Sharp and Vaughan Williams to lecture to it.

Then, on 6 December 1911, the English Folk Dance Society was formed at a public meeting in St Andrews Hall, Newman Street, London W1. Butterworth was an active member from the start, served on the committee in the early days, and remained a member to the end of his life. The EFDS was led by Sharp, who had a close band of associates, including Butterworth, although there was a certain rivalry from Mary Neal's Espérance Working Girls' Club, the activities of which included music, dancing and acting. 'Mary' Neal (born Clara Sophia) (1860–1944) formed this club in 1895 and first met

Sharp ten years later. At first, they worked in close harmony, but from 1908 relationships were strained and they appeared together for the last time in January 1909, in Cambridge. Disagreements on how folk-dancing should be taught, and on how the whole folk-dancing revival should be developed, continued for several years. Sharp did not support Neal's ideas, and she did not seek out his experience and skill in these matters; he had the knowledge and musicianship she lacked, making up for it through her organising ability and general enthusiasm. Sharp was bitterly disappointed that the collaboration failed. In 1909, he established a 'School of Morris Dancing' at the South-Western Polytechnic Institute in Chelsea, where the teachers included Maud Karpeles and her sister Helen, who later married Douglas Kennedy, a leading figure in folk-dancing from these early days until 1987, the year of his death. It was here that Kennedy met Butterworth, and he remained a close friend until 1916. The Karpeles sisters later started the Folk Dance Club at their home in Bayswater, and this led eventually to the formation of the EFDS in 1911.[1] Rivalry continued between Sharp and Neal up to the outbreak of war in 1914, when the Espérance Club 'pursued an independent programme with perhaps more colourful displays, which we [the EFDS] considered flamboyant'.[2] Yet not all was antagonistic, as Douglas Kennedy remembered giving a private lesson on the jig, *I'll go and enlist for a sailor,* to Neville Lytton, one of the Club's best dancers. The Club gradually disintegrated during the War and never recovered, although Mary Neal was awarded the CBE in 1937, for services in connection with the revival of folksongs and -dances. The EFDS survived the War, and has

---

[1] For a detailed account of the founding of the EFDS, *cf.* Derek Schofield, ' "Revival of the Folk Dance: An Artistic Movement": The Background of the Founding of the English Folk Dance Society in 1911', *Folk Music Journal,* Vol. 5, No. 7, 1986, pp. 215–19.

[2] Letter from Douglas Kennedy to the author, 3 January 1981. I am much indebted to the late Mr Kennedy for information concerning the early days of the EFDS.

Cecil Sharp (courtesy of the English Folk Dance and Song Society

flourished ever since, despite some doubt as to its continuation after Sharp's death in 1924.

The first president of the EFDS, in 1912, was Lady (Mary) Trefusis (née Lygon), who played an important part in the Society's affairs. She is perhaps best remembered as a possible subject of the thirteenth of Elgar's *Enigma Variations*, the lady on a sea voyage.[3] Elgar himself had attended the first AGM of the Folk Song Society in 1899, 'moved the adoption of the committee's report, and [so] both opened and closed

---

[3] For a discussion on this matter, *cf.* Nicholas Reed, 'Elgar's Enigmatic Inamorata', *The Musical Times*, Vol. cxxv, No. 1698, August 1984, pp. 430–34.

his connection with the folksong revival'.[4] He believed that a composer's job was to invent tunes, not to borrow and elaborate on them.

Butterworth was an excellent dancer and exponent of intricate dance movements, and he held a prominent position in the original men's morris side, which made its first public appearance in late February 1912 (both the 22nd and 27th have been quoted) at the Suffolk Street Galleries, London. The other members of the side were Douglas Kennedy, A. Claude Wright,[5] James Paterson,[6] Perceval Lucas[7] and George Jerrard Wilkinson.[8] Another member of the side, although not a regular one, was R. J. E. Tiddy.[9] Such was the skill and reputation of this side that it gave the first stage performance of folk-dancing on 2 December 1912 at the Savoy Theatre. This event was prompted by Harley Granville Barker, who had the use of the theatre for his season of

[4] Michael Kennedy, *Portrait of Elgar*, Oxford University Press, Oxford and London, 3rd edn. (1987), p. 104 (1st edn. 1968, 2nd edn. 1982).

[5] Wright eventually became an Air Commodore in the RAF before his retirement.

[6] Paterson, a Birmingham man, worked closely with King George VI on Boys' Camps.

[7] Lucas was the younger brother of E. V. Lucas, the author of travel books, and edited the first two numbers of the *EFDS Journal*, before his untimely death at the Somme. Sharp remarked that he was 'the first man who really understood what folkdance revival meant' (Maud Karpeles, *Cecil Sharp, His Life and Work*, Routledge & Kegan Paul, London, 1967, p. 117).

[8] Wilkinson (1885–1916), a Cambridge graduate and a composer of songs, succeeded Sharp at Ludgrove Preparatory School, Barnet, where Sharp was music master from 1893 to 1910. He became a close friend of Butterworth, and was killed at the Somme five weeks before him, on 1 July 1916. For more details on Wilkinson, *cf.* A. C. Rankin, 'George Jerrard Wilkinson', *The British Music Society Newsletter*, No. 4, Winter 1979, pp. 9–11.

[9] Tiddy (1879–1916), another Somme victim, was killed five days after Butterworth. He was a Fellow of Trinity College, Oxford, and a lecturer in English and Classical Literature. His full name, Reginald John Elliot Tiddy, must have confused John Rippin, who refers to a 'Reginald Elliot' (*loc. cit.*, p. 681).

*The first men's side of the English Folk Dance Society: Douglas Kennedy,
Butterworth, James Paterson, Perceval Lucas, A. Claude Wright
and George Jerrard Wilkinson (courtesy of D. Rowe)*

Shakespeare. Only two performances were given, a matinee
and an evening. Douglas Kennedy recalled that after the
matinee

> George took some of us round to the Savoy Hotel for tea, and,
> of course, we looked dreadful still half-attired in our dance
> costumes. We were met by a flunkey, who suggested we try one
> of the cafés in the Strand. George then showed his mettle by
> showing us to a table himself, and withered the flunkey with a
> reference to ourselves as super-employees of the Savoy.[10]

For the two and a half years up to the outbreak of war,
there were very few weekends when the morris sides were not
involved in dancing, usually to illustrate Sharp's Saturday
lecture-demonstrations at schools and colleges, and Sharp
'was prepared to visit any town that would give him a public

[10] Letter from Douglas Kennedy to the author, dated 3 January 1981;
cf. also Appendix Four, pp. 166–68.

hearing'.[11] Courses of a week's duration were held at Stratford-on-Avon each Christmas and summer until war broke out, including a summer school in August 1911 (*before* the EFDS was founded), which lasted four weeks. At one of these courses, Butterworth remarked that it was one of the few occasions when he had lived in a 'really musical atmosphere'.[12]

At a course held in August 1912, the demonstration team was filmed in Stratford High Street, the film being shown in Pathé's *Animated Gazette*, but there remains no trace of it now. More important are the 'Kinora' spools of film depicting Sharp, Butterworth and the Karpeles sisters demonstrating various dances. (The Kinora was a primitive type of home movie.) One spool was sent to a relative of Butterworth (a Miss Wigan – a cousin from Portishead?) shortly after his death, and it remained with the family until 1972, when it was given to the Bodleian Library, Oxford; in the catalogue there, it is described as a 'flickbook showing George Butterworth dancing'.

In the early 1980s, five more Kinora spools were discovered at Cecil Sharp House in London (the home of the English Folk Dance and Song Society), and again these films showed Butterworth and others dancing. To obtain the best results, all six spools were transferred to cine film and later to videotape. They were all taken on the same occasion, most probably on 20 June 1912, when it is known that the team was demonstrating at a fete in Kelmscot, near Faringdon, Oxfordshire. Of the five recently discovered films, three show the Karpeles sisters, another Butterworth dancing the Field Town Morris Jig, *Molly Oxford*, and a fifth all four dancers in *Hey Boys Up Go We*, which may well be the only film of Sharp dancing. The Bodleian Kinora shows Butterworth dancing the complex jig *I'll go and enlist for a sailor*, and this film was

---

[11] Douglas Kennedy, 'Tradition', *Folk Music Journal*, Vol. 4, No. 3, 1982, p. 196.

[12] Quoted in Maud Karpeles, *op. cit.*, p. 85. Butterworth was folk-dancing at Stratford when war broke out.

Cecil Sharp, Maud and Helen Karpeles and Butterworth
dancing Hey Boys Up Go We
(courtesy of the English Folk Dance and Song Society)

'clearly intended as a demonstration for instructional purposes; now, seventy years on, it can at last be used'.[13]

Apart from a busy schedule of demonstrations in this
country, the team also paid two visits abroad: Paris (June
1913) and Brussels (early in 1914). Douglas Kennedy recalled
that the Brussels expedition

> was as part of a live exhibition of M. Poiret's dress designs, and
> we were being used as a 'turn' to contrast with the Poiret
> costumes and the mannequins. The audience were a rich
> section of the upper crust and, even so, they showed much
> enthusiasm.[14]

---

[13] For detailed descriptions of these early films, *cf.* two fascinating articles
by Mike Heaney: 'Films from the Past', *English Dance and Song*, Vol. 45,
No. 3, Autumn/Winter 1983, pp. 20–21; and 'Butterworth Dancing', *The
Morris Dancer*, No. 15, March 1983, pp. 7–12.

[14] Letter from Douglas Kennedy to the author, dated 3 January 1981.

The dancers on this occasion comprised a team of six men and their partners, under Sharp's direction, with the violinist Elsie ('Ruby') Avril, who later became an important member of the Society. The Paris demonstration was more conventional, with a similar team of dancers; an attempt to film the team was unsuccessful.

Butterworth's important contribution to the early collection of folksongs was spread over a number of years (1906–13), the most fruitful period being the summer of 1907. At this and at other times he travelled extensively throughout England, collecting songs from Sussex (his most productive county), Kent, Monmouthshire, Oxfordshire, Berkshire, Hampshire, Buckinghamshire, Norfolk, Suffolk, Herefordshire, Shropshire and Yorkshire. In 1912 and 1913, Butterworth and Sharp collected morris dances in the Midlands and sword dances in the North-East.

As a folksong collector, Butterworth was versatile, fastidious and painstaking; in this work he sometimes collaborated with Francis Jekyll and Vaughan Williams. Jekyll, a relatively obscure figure in the folksong revival, was three years Butterworth's senior and, similarly, educated at Eton and Oxford. He, too, became a member of the FSS, and joined the EFDS at its inauguration in 1911.[15] Together they made spasmodic collections of songs between September 1906 and November 1910, chiefly in Sussex (1908) and Norfolk (1910). After Butterworth's death, Jekyll wrote: 'Some of my happiest days were those which we spent together, tramping the Sussex Downs and collecting songs.'[16]

Folk Songs from Sussex
One collection of folksong arrangements published during Butterworth's lifetime was *Folk Songs from Sussex*. Each of the eleven songs, mostly arranged between 1906 and 1909, is given a simple, delightful and musical accompaniment,

[15] Jekyll collected 57 songs, including some from Warwickshire, Kent and Hampshire, without Butterworth's collaboration.

[16] *Scrapbook*, f. 73.

revealing the hand of a natural composer, and they may be regarded as preliminary studies for the Housman settings and other songs; some of Sharp's arrangements are, in comparison, rather pedestrian. In the 1974 republication, Jekyll has no mention, although it was he who noted down four of the songs.

Butterworth's preface to these folksongs is dated 30 June 1912, and the set was published the following year:

1. *Yonder stands a lovely creature.* Jekyll noted this tune, a good example of one known in several different versions (e.g., *No, John, no*).

2. *A blacksmith courted me.*

3. *Sowing the seeds of love.* This tune was Sharp's earliest find, in Hambridge, Somerset, in September 1903.

4. *A lawyer he went out.* Noted by Jekyll, this tune also appears as the last song of *Summer*, in Vaughan Williams' *Folk Songs of the Four Seasons*, where it is called *The Green Meadow.*

5. *Come my own one.* This arrangement is particularly fine, and was at one time published separately in a lower key.

6. *The cuckoo.* The words of this song are well-known, and are often to be found in collections of school songs, but to a different tune. This melody has a delightful major/minor conflict.

7. *A brisk young sailor courted me.* This version of the tune is that noted by Jekyll in 1908 at Scaynes Hill, although Butterworth also noted the song some twenty miles away at Billingshurst, with considerable melodic differences, in July 1909.[17]

8. *Seventeen come Sunday.* Vaughan Williams made use of this tune in his *English Folk-Song Suite*, for military band (later orchestrated by Gordon Jacob).

9. *Roving in the dew.* This well-known song, like *Come my own one*, was also published separately. Butterworth's arrangement dates from June 1907 although, a year earlier, Jekyll

---

[17] For a comparison of the two versions, *cf.* Michael Dawney, 'George Butterworth's Folk Music Manuscripts', *Folk Music Journal*, Vol. 3, No. 2, 1976, pp. 105–6.

had also noted the tune, with several melodic variations, and it is his version that appears in the first of the *Two English Idylls* (Ex. 29). Here, and in Dunhill's arrangement for unison voices, the song is called *Dabbling in the dew*.

Ex. 29

(a)   Jekyll

(b)   Butterworth

10. *The true lover's farewell* (or *The turtle dove*). The simple accompaniment consists entirely of chord progressions, leading, somewhat surprisingly, to big C minor chords at the end, which seem a little out of place in straightforward folksong arrangements. This song, too, was published separately and was likewise arranged by Vaughan Williams.

11. *Tarry Trowsers.* Jekyll noted this tune, to which reference is made in the first movement of Vaughan Williams' *A Sea Symphony*.[18]

Butterworth also collected songs with Vaughan Williams, although the number they noted jointly amounts to little more than twenty. Vaughan Williams himself collected his

---

[18]   *Cf.* p. 7 of the vocal score, at the *allegro* section.

first song, *Bushes and Briars*, from an old shepherd near
Brentwood, Essex, in December 1903, only three months
after Sharp had heard his first folksong. In all, Vaughan
Williams accumulated 810 songs, including more than 230 in
1904 alone, mostly from East Anglia, the home counties,
Sussex and Herefordshire. Somerset, Sharp's main area, and
most other western counties, he avoided. In fact, it was not
Sharp but Lucy Broadwood (1858–1929), one of the
founders of the Folk Song Society, who first drew Vaughan
Williams' attention to folksong. Vaughan Williams and
Butterworth did not collaborate in folksong collecting until
October 1910, when a trip was made to East Anglia, in
particular to the Southwold area of Suffolk and the Norfolk
Broads; a second visit to East Anglia took place in December
1911, when their activities centred on Diss, on the Norfolk-
Suffolk border. Michael Dawney[19] points out that a number
of the songs exist in both composers' manuscripts, with a
further seven in Vaughan Williams' only, although they were
jointly collected. Folksong collecting was not without its
amusing moments, and Ursula Vaughan Williams relates an
incident which befell the two composers in East Anglia.[20]

---

[19] *Loc. cit.*, p. 100.

[20] 'One night, in a pub where they had found several singers, one of them
suggested it would be much quicker if he rowed them across the water than
that they should bicycle round the Broad by road. It was a brilliantly starry
night, frosty and still. They piled their bicycles into the boat and started.
Their ferryman rowed with uncertain strokes, raising his oar now and then
to point at distant lights, saying "Lowestoft" or "Southwold". Before long
they realized they were always the same lights and that he was taking them
round and round in circles. The night air after the frowsty bar parlour and
the beer had been fatal, and he was thoroughly drunk. Eventually they
persuaded him to let them row. Luck guided them to a jetty among the
reeds. By this time their singer was sound asleep and did not wake even
when they extricated their bicycles from under him. So they tied the boat
up and left him there while they bicycled down an unknown track and
found their way back to Southwold. The singer survived and was found in
the same pub the next evening. But this time they did not accept his offer
of a short cut by water' (*R.V.W.: A Portrait of Ralph Vaughan Williams*, Oxford
University Press, Oxford and London, 1964 (paperback edn. 1988),
pp. 98–99).

Butterworth left most of his manuscripts to Vaughan Williams, who presented the folksong collections to Cecil Sharp House in 1937. It was nearly forty years later that Michael Dawney began to edit Butterworth's collection of folk songs and, from this research, it transpired that he had collected nearly 300 songs, as well as numerous dances. Of the songs, over half contain no words, a good number exist complete, while others remain in fragmentary form or exist with words only.[21] Dawney's concise and informative article[22] is invaluable in its acknowledgement of Butterworth as one of Britain's most important folksong collectors.

Apart from *Folk Songs from Sussex*, Butterworth published many others, in the *Journal of the Folk Song Society*.[23] He also submitted a further 25 songs for publication, but these were rejected either on the grounds that they did not conform to what were then regarded as 'folksongs' or because similar versions of the same songs had already appeared in the *Journal*. In 1977, the EFDSS (which had come into being with the merger of the FSS and EFDS in 1932) published some 'hitherto unpublished' songs from Butterworth's collection, in a volume entitled *The Ploughboy's Glory*, edited by Michael Dawney.

An illuminating account of the rivalry which existed between Mary Neal's Espérance Club and Sharp's followers in the EFDS is portrayed in letters written by Miss Dorothy Marshall, from Petersfield, to Clive Carey, about folksong and dance collecting in Sussex and Hampshire.[24] Carey (1883–1968), a well-known singer, teacher and opera producer, also a composer of songs, and a close friend of W. Denis Browne, Edward Dent and Armstrong Gibbs,

---

[21] *Cf.* pp. 147–63 for a list of Butterworth's folksongs.

[22] *Loc. cit.*, pp. 99–113.

[23] *Cf.* Vol. IV, No. 15, December 1910 and, more especially, Vol. IV, No. 17, January 1913.

[24] Frank Howes, 'Letters to Clive Carey', *English Dance and Song*, Vol. 33, No. 2, Summer 1971, pp. 65–66. *Cf.* also a recent article on the Espérance movement: Roy Judge, 'Mary Neal and the Espérance Morris', *Folk Music Journal*, Vol. 5, No. 5, 1989, pp. 545–91.

became Mary Neal's musical adviser in 1908, taking over from
Herbert MacIlwaine, Sharp's collaborator in *The Morris Book.*
Carey preserved these letters, dating from 1911 to 1913, and
in them it is interesting to note Miss Marshall's references to
Butterworth, whom she came across in similar work. On
22 September 1911, 'Mr Butterworth was none too pleased to
find me there [at the Workhouse with a phonograph for
recording] before him'. Less than a week later he had
become 'the egregious Butterworth' and, before another two
weeks had passed, she asked if Carey knew Frederick Keel,[25]
and whether he was 'an improvement on Mr Butterworth'.
Carey was one of several assiduous song-collectors in Sussex
in the early years of this century, and his achievements have
been compared with Butterworth's, Carey accumulating far
more texts than tunes (236 to 108) whereas with Butterworth
the reverse was the case (53 to 129).[26] This second figure
suggests some exaggeration on the part of Lucy Broadwood,
when recalling her first meeting with Butterworth, 'his arms
full of some hundreds of songs that he had collected in [...]
Sussex'.[27] In fact, many of the early collectors were more
interested in the tunes than in the words or the singers
themselves whereas, for the singers themselves, words and
tune were of equal importance.

On Christmas Night, We get up in the morn
and In the Highlands

In 1912 Butterworth arranged two other traditional tunes, *On
Christmas Night* and *We get up in the morn.* The first is an old
English carol melody, adapted for four-part choir, but now
completely overshadowed by Vaughan Williams' version. It is
another Sussex tune, noted by Butterworth in April 1907. *We*

---

[25] Keel (1871–1954) was secretary of the Folk Song Society from 1911 to
1919, and editor of the *Journal.* He also composed songs, of which *Trade
Winds* is the best-known.

[26] Vic Gammon, 'Folk-song Collecting in Sussex and Surrey, 1843–1914',
History Workshop Journal, Vol. 10, Autumn 1980, pp. 61–89.

[27] Letter to Lady Butterworth, 16 March 1917 (*Scrapbook,* ff. 82–83).

get up in the morn is a harvest song, arranged for four-part male chorus, and Butterworth's setting is a lively one. The first verse has each part entering at two bars' distance, while the other verses are largely homophonic, the final stanza working up to an impressive climax (Ex. 30).

Ex. 30

Another short choral work, not connected with folksong, may be mentioned here: *In the Highlands*, a setting for female voices and piano of words by R. L. Stevenson. It, too, dates from 1912 and, as these three short works comprise Butterworth's entire choral output, it is convenient to discuss them together. *In the Highlands*, which was also set as a choral piece by Cyril Rootham, is an apt illustration of Stevenson's evocation of the countryside, Butterworth achieving a successful result through variety and unity of musical content, not least by way of a piano accompaniment of some significance (Ex. 31).

Ex. 31

In the collection of morris dances Butterworth collaborated with Cecil Sharp. Although only a relatively small percentage of the songs was printed, the majority of the dances were published, some in *The Morris Book* and in *Morris Dance Tunes*;[28] Butterworth was involved also in some sections of the *Country Dance Book*.[29]

Sharp had begun to collect dances as early as December 1899, at Headington, near Oxford, when morris dancers visited the house of some relatives with whom he was staying; later he collected the tunes to which the dances were performed. Butterworth began to assist Sharp in this work in 1912, in and around Oxfordshire. The dances performed were grouped under the names of the various villages where the steps and tunes had been noted: thus those at Bledington, on the Oxfordshire-Gloucestershire border,

---

[28] *The Morris Book* ('A History of Morris Dancing, with a Description of Dances as performed by the Morris-men of England'), Novello, London, 1907 (Part 1, revised 1912), 1909 (Part 2), 1910 (Part 3), 1911 (Part 4), 1913 (Part 5); reprinted by E. P. Publishing Ltd, Wakefield, 1974 (Parts 1–3), 1975 (Parts 4 and 5); and subsequently by A. & C. Black and Harry Styles (*cf.* Appendix Three, p. 164). For the first three parts, Sharp was assisted by Herbert MacIlwaine, Musical Director of the Espérance Club from 1901 to 1908. Part 1 was first dedicated to Espérance girls and carried an introduction by MacIlwaine; the 1912 revised edition has neither dedication nor introduction. Part 4 was entirely Sharp's work, MacIlwaine not having the time to give assistance, although, in truth, the role he played in preparing Part 3 was negligible. Butterworth collaborated with Sharp in Part 5.
Morris Dance Tunes, Novello, London, 1907–13. There are ten books, Butterworth and Sharp being responsible for the last two (1913).

[29] Novello, London, 1909–22. There were later editions and revisions until E. P. Publishing Ltd, Wakefield, reprinted the entire collection in three stages, Parts 1 and 2 (1972), Parts 3 and 4 (1975), Parts 5 and 6 (1976). Later, A. & C. Black and, more recently, Harry Styles acquired the rights to publish these volumes (*cf.* Appendix Three, p. 164). Sharp was involved in all six parts, with assistance from Butterworth (Parts 3 and 4) and Maud Karpeles (Part 5). Parts 3 and 4 (1912 and 1916) were issued in connection with *Country Dance Tunes* (Novello, London, 1912), Sets 5–8, and contain 35 (Part 3) and 45 (Part 4) country dances from *The English Dancing Master* (1650–70), described by Butterworth and Sharp.

were known as the Bledington tradition. Butterworth found one tradition himself, at Badby, in Northamptonshire. In making these dances generally known, Sharp was somewhat handicapped by the lack of an accepted system of dance notation, although one of the most renowned (and oldest) systems of the past (Thoinot Arbeau's *Orchésographie* of 1588) gave him

> the idea of indicating the timing of the steps by showing on which notes of the accompanying melody they fall. In his Morris Dance books, the movements are shown by printing under the melody a line of abbreviated symbols for the steps and a lower line for the track, whilst the hand-movements are placed above the melody.[30]

Butterworth also arranged some of the tunes for piano, but only in a way which satisfied him as a musician; he later discovered that his arrangements were not at all suitable as accompaniments to the dances, and that

> the only satisfactory solution was to scrap them and adopt Cecil Sharp's method. This he did with such success that Cecil Sharp himself could not later remember which were his own arrangements and which were George Butterworth's.[31]

One of Butterworth's most outstanding achievements in this field lay in his own quest for dances in and around Bicester in April 1912, details of which he kept in a diary, which remained unpublished for 65 years.[32] This important document reveals much of his pioneer work in a rather remote part of the rural Midlands; it includes the earliest existing notes on all four of the set dances which were later published in *The Morris Book*, Part 5. Between 13 and 24 April 1912, Butterworth remained in the Bicester area, taking

---

[30] Maud Karpeles, *op. cit.*, p. 107.

[31] *Ibid.*, p. 108.

[32] Russell Wortley and Michael Dawney (eds.), 'George Butterworth's Diary of Morris Dance Hunting', *Folk Music Journal*, Vol. 3, No. 3, 1977, pp. 193–207.

pains to extricate details of various traditions in the surrounding villages, and, in particular, the Bucknell Morris.[33] His work began after a visit to relatives at Portishead, and the diary relates the frustrations and excitements of these few days. It was certainly hard work, as many of the old inhabitants supplied unreliable information, or played tunes so badly that it was difficult for Butterworth to write anything down. In some villages, the morris had not been danced for up to fifty years, and there were relatively few survivors anywhere.

Yet Butterworth did manage to glean some useful information about traditions that were gradually dying out. Reginald Lennard, his friend from Oxford days, accompanied him several times in search of morris dances, and recalled that Butterworth had 'a genius for avoiding a false scent'.[34] Lennard once found the composer at work in an old cottage at Bucknell, noting dances from a very old man, who stumbled his way through long disused and half-forgotten steps, and then, with his brother, capering through the morris along the village street, accompanied by pipe and tabor, while Butterworth, with a pile of notebooks, and oblivious of all, calmly noted down details of these dances.[35] The old men appeared most grateful to find Butterworth so interested in their craft. The Bucknell Morris certainly lasted longer than most, even up to 1911, at the time of King George V's coronation. In spite of this discovery, Butterworth was somewhat disappointed, the dancers 'merely adumbrating the steps. Some [...] are quite clear, others unintelligible, and the joins are bad'.[36] On more than one occasion the diary

---

[33] For a detailed description of the Bucknell Morris, *cf.* Russell Wortley, 'The Bucknell Morris', *English Dance and Song*, Vol. 41, No. 2, 1979, pp. 12–14.

[34] *Memorial Volume*, p. 97.

[35] These were two of the Rolfe brothers, Eli and Will, with Joe Powell on pipe and tabor.

[36] Quoted in Wortley and Dawney, *loc. cit.*, p. 200.

The Bucknell Morris in 1875
(courtesy of the English Folk Dance and Song Society)

reveals that he decided not to do anything further at Bucknell 'until after seeing Sharp'.

Another description of the same performers appears in a book by E. V. Lucas, in which the author accompanied Sharp (referred to as 'The Director') to Bucknell (although Lucas does not name the village) shortly after Butterworth's visit.[37]

In July 1912, Butterworth was again in Oxfordshire, collecting dances at Filkins – on the Gloucestershire border, near Lechlade – where he noted down eight tunes from a John Pougher, each of them a version of well-known melodies found in various localities.[38]

Shortly after these Oxfordshire visits, Sharp and Butterworth went to a rather different part of England, the

[37] *London Lavender*, Methuen, London, 1912, pp. 220–24.

[38] For a detailed description of these tunes and dances, *cf.* Philip S. Heath-Coleman, 'Morris Dancing at Filkins', *English Dance and Song*, Vol. 44, No. 1, Spring 1982, pp. 14–16. *Cf.* also p. 145.

North-East, to collect sword dances among the industrial communities, Sharp publishing them in three volumes.[39] Douglas Kennedy recalls[40] that, while collecting and describing these dances, Sharp

> had become dulled to the atmosphere of controlled power and underlying fire, so [. . . that] he failed at first to give us the picture of this local tradition in all its dynamism.

Butterworth, he goes on,

> was more successful, and struggled to give us the style and manner of stepping, but he never quite set us alight so our own performance for long remained pedestrian.

With Butterworth's own considerable ability as a dancer, he and Sharp were undoubtedly the finest exponents, although Butterworth was the model example for all to follow, being younger and fitter than Sharp, and equally well-versed in the morris. Wortley[41] remembers being told by Douglas Kennedy that Butterworth claimed to be the only person able to dance the very intricate double caper properly; this was around 1913. The importance Butterworth attached to his skill as a dancer becomes obvious when, in conversation with Lennard, who had spoken of him as a musician, Butterworth protested, 'I'm not a musician, I'm a professional dancer'.[42]

What, then, is Butterworth's position in the folksong revival? Numerically, of course, he was overshadowed by Vaughan Williams (810 songs collected) and Sharp (about 3,300 songs in England alone) but, largely due to Michael Dawney's sterling work, Butterworth's achievement can now

---

[39] Cecil Sharp, *The Sword Dances of Northern England*, Novello, London, 1911–13 (2nd edn., 1950–51, edited by Maud Karpeles).

[40] *Loc. cit.*, p. 198.

[41] *Loc. cit.*, p. 13.

[42] *George Butterworth – The Man and His Music*, BBC Home Service, 14 July 1942.

Cecil Sharp and troupe at Burford, 1913; Butterworth is standing in the back row, far right (courtesy of the English Folk Dance and Song Society)

be placed more accurately in perspective; with his thorough-going research and true musicianship, he must surely rank as one of the foremost collectors of English folksongs.

Sharp and Butterworth had very similar views and ideals and, as Sharp was the leading force behind the English folksong revival, a certain amount of criticism has been levelled against him, on two counts in particular: his out-of-date methods and his general principles.

Certainly, by Eastern European and North American standards, the methods of collectors of English folksong, with the sole exception of Percy Grainger, were behind the times. In the 1890s sound recordings were made in Russia (by Evgeniya Lineva in 1897), North America (by Dr Walter Fewkes in 1899), New Zealand, Hungary and Tasmania, and in 1906, when Bartók began his work, he considered the phonograph essential (he may well have been influenced by Grainger). Until 1906, English folksong collectors had noted songs by hand, but in that year Percy Grainger, practical as

Cecil Sharp and troupe at Stratford, 1914; Butterworth is second from the left in the back row (courtesy of the English Folk Dance and Song Society)

ever, began using a phonograph in Lincolnshire to record all his songs, over 200 of which survive. He was the first person in Western Europe to do so, probably taking the idea from Hjalmar Thuren's work in the Faeroe Islands in 1901. Thuren was an authority on Danish folklore and had met Grainger in Denmark in 1905. Sharp took down the majority of his songs by hand but, following Grainger's example, did experiment with the phonograph from 1907, although he was never wholly convinced of its advantages.[43] There is little

---

[43] In a letter to Grainger, Sharp set out his objections to using the gramophone, in particular that 'in transmitting a song, our aim should be to record its artistic effect, not necessarily the exact means by which that effect was produced' (quoted in *Music from the People*, BBC Radio 4, 26 June 1985). Grainger had little time for Sharp's method of collecting folksongs – his view was that songs should be noted down exactly from what was heard, not from what he thought ought to have been sung. There is now no doubt that Grainger's achievements in the folksong revival were considerable, but in his day his ideas and innovations were most controversial, and only in recent years has his true stature as a folklorist been revealed.

Butterworth dancing a jig at Burford in 1913
(courtesy of the English Folk Dance and Song Society)

evidence that Butterworth used a recording machine,
although there are references to two songs (*New Garden Fields*
and *Lovely Joan*), collected by him and Vaughan Williams in
October 1910, when a phonograph appears to have been
used.[44] Fewer than twenty of Vaughan Williams' vast collection of folksongs were recorded by phonograph, such was his
aversion to all things mechanical; that he did experiment
with a recording machine (from 1909) was undoubtedly due
to Grainger's influence and his characteristic drive and
enthusiasm for anything new.

[44] *Folk Song Society Journal*, Vol. 4, No. 17, January 1913, p. 334, for *New
Garden Fields*; Michael Kennedy, *The Works of Ralph Vaughan Williams*,
Oxford University Press, 1964 (2nd edn. of catalogue, 1982), for *Lovely
Joan*.

Sharp's principles and ultimate aims have been con-demned as one-sided by some folklorists, especially the late A. L. Lloyd whose Marxist standpoint in folklore studies was a far cry from Sharp's. Lloyd believed that Sharp's view of the singers who provided the songs as 'noble, unlettered prim-itives, snug in their thatched cottages, far from the wicked cities', was quite mistaken and that the country-dwellers had been transformed from 'a peasantry into an agricultural proletariat, and Somerset, Sharp's main stamping-ground, was one of the worst examples'. Sharp's theory that folksongs will do 'incalculable good in civilising the masses' did not appeal to the working classes, who 'rejected the notion of folksong adapted to middle-class standards and imposed officially from above'.[45]

It is true that Sharp, Butterworth and others presented a somewhat one-sided view of the British folksong heritage, concentrating almost exclusively on rural England, with very little indication of what was a flourishing aspect of folklore in towns and cities. Nevertheless, one cannot deny all the work they did achieve at the beginning of this century, and the vast heritage of folksongs and dances they discovered for others to enjoy.

What did the folksong revival mean to composers in England, and how much was Butterworth influenced by the way others made use of folk material in their music? Folksong influence can readily be discerned in the melodic lines and accom-paniments of songs by Butterworth and Vaughan Williams – but what, for example, of the use of folk material in orchestral works?

Such pieces by Butterworth (*Two English Idylls, A Shropshire Lad* Rhapsody – although it does not quote a folktune – and *The Banks of Green Willow*) date from the years 1910–13, several years after Vaughan Williams' first essays in similar vein, *In the Fen Country* (completed in 1904) and the three

[45] A. L. Lloyd, *Folk Song and the Collectors*, BBC Radio 3, 26 September 1983.

Sharp's Morris team at Burford; Butterworth is second on the right
(courtesy of the English Folk Dance and Song Society)

Norfolk Rhapsodies (1905/6). In addition, there are such works as Holst's *A Somerset Rhapsody* (1906/7) and Delius' *Brigg Fair* (1907), although the latter, a more organised set of variations on a theme, is less readily comparable to Butterworth's achievements in this field. It is possible, of course, that Butterworth may have had the opportunity to hear one or more of these orchestral works, especially *In the Fen Country* (first performed in February 1909 at the Queen's Hall under Beecham) and the first *Norfolk Rhapsody* (first heard in August 1906, also at the Queen's Hall, with Henry Wood conducting), and thus learn something of the methods employed by other composers when using folktunes within the context of an orchestral work.

Of the *Norfolk Rhapsodies*, indeed, only the first was published, and that in a quite extensive revision of 1914, after Vaughan Williams' studies with Ravel. Little is known of the other Rhapsodies – they were premiered in Cardiff in September 1907 by the composer, and London first heard them in April 1912 under Balfour Gardiner (Butterworth could have attended this particular concert), but apparently they have not been performed since 1914.

Butterworth around 1911, the year in which he completed
Six Songs from 'A Shropshire Lad' *and in which he*
became a founder member of the English Folk Dance Society
(courtesy of the Provost and Fellows of Eton College)

In the first *Norfolk Rhapsody*, the chief theme is *The Captain's Apprentice*, collected at King's Lynn in January 1905, almost six years before Butterworth (together with Vaughan Williams) came across it in another part of Norfolk.

According to Vaughan Williams, the effect of the folksong revival on English composers was such that

> we were dazzled, we wanted to preach a new gospel, we wanted to rhapsodize on these tunes just as Liszt and Grieg had done on theirs. [...] we simply were fascinated by the tunes and wanted other people to be fascinated too, and our mentors in the public press have lost no opportunity of telling us so.[46]

---

[46] Ralph Vaughan Williams, *National Music and Other Essays*, Oxford University Press, Oxford and London, 1963 (2nd edn. 1987), p. 46.

V

A SHROPSHIRE LAD RHAPSODY AND OTHER WORKS

In the later years of his folksong collecting, Butterworth composed two exquisite examples of orchestral music, the Rhapsody, *A Shropshire Lad*, and the Idyll, *The Banks of Green Willow*, both bearing the imprint of folksong, either directly or indirectly. He also wrote at this time two works which veered away from folksong, the song-cycle *Love Blows as the Wind Blows* and the incomplete orchestral *Fantasia*.

Rhapsody, *A Shropshire Lad*

Without doubt Butterworth's finest achievement is the orchestral Rhapsody, *A Shropshire Lad*, sketches for which were most likely begun during his year at Radley (1909–10). In his customary manner, a long time was spent carefully revising the work, so that the final score was not ready until 1911. Another two years passed before the first performance, and four more before it was published. Even the title proved problematical. Butterworth first favoured 'Orchestral Prelude, *The Land of Lost Content*' then 'Orchestral Prelude *The Cherry Tree*', before, relatively late, settling on its final name. These titles evidently confused both Edward Lockspeiser and Harvey Grace, who believed *The Cherry Tree* to be a separate work.[1]

In spite of the long period from conception to publication, the Rhapsody has proved, over the decades, to be Butter-

---

[1] Lockspeiser, 'Mixed Gallery', in A. L. Bacharach (ed.) *British Music of Our Time*, Pelican Books, Harmondsworth, 1946, p. 193; Grace,'Butterworth

worth's greatest work and has never been neglected. The inspiration obviously sprang from the earlier song-cycle, but there is no doubt that, notwithstanding many fine points in the vocal work, the Rhapsody shows evidence of an even bigger talent; indeed, it seems to be on a higher plane than anything he had composed up to that time.

Butterworth described the Rhapsody as being

> in the nature of an orchestral epilogue to [my] two sets of *Shropshire Lad* songs; the thematic material is chiefly derived from the melody of [...] *Loveliest of trees*, but otherwise no connection is to be inferred with the words of the song. The intention of the Rhapsody is rather to express the home-thoughts of the exiled 'Shropshire Lad'.[2]

The elegiac and pastoral music thus created by Butterworth was very much of its time, an example of what the late Christopher Palmer has called 'a threnody for the passing of the good life, [...] for those [...] glorious Edwardian summers'.[3] Many English works dating from around this time convey a similar mood to that of the Rhapsody: Vaughan Williams' *Pastoral Symphony* (1922), Finzi's *Severn Rhapsody* (1923) and some of the early instrumental works of Howells

---

and the Folksong Revival', *The Listener*, Vol. xxviii, No. 704, 9 July 1942, p. 61.

Butterworth sent a brief analysis of the work to Herbert Thompson, the Yorkshire music critic, on 3 June 1913, four months before the first performance. Here it is called *The Cherry Tree*, the title having 'no more concern with cherry trees than with beetles'. In a later letter to Thompson, dating from late summer 1913, Butterworth gives his final preference for the title 'Rhapsody', after having pondered over various other titles for the work. In a third letter, dated 9 June 1913 (six days after the first), Butterworth almost regrets sending Thompson the analysis of a work of 'very small proportions'. The first two of these letters (written in Oxford) are quoted in Lewis Foreman, *From Parry to Britten*, Batsford, London, 1987, pp. 55–56, and all three are to be found in the Herbert Thompson collection at Leeds University (MS. 361).

[2] Programme note by the composer for the first London performance, on 20 March 1914; reprinted in *Memorial Volume*, p. 114.

[3] *Herbert Howells: A Study*, Novello, 1978, p. 23.

are among the best examples. The poignant and expressive
ideas in the music of the Rhapsody are all the more moving
when one considers that, within a few years, war had claimed
its composer and many of his friends.

The Rhapsody requires large orchestral forces, including
cor anglais, bass clarinet and harp, although one outstanding
feature is the delicacy of much of the orchestration, Butterworth employing his full resources only in the central
climax.

The work opens with a hushed A minor chord on muted
strings, above which a haunting four-note figure in thirds
alternates between violas and clarinets (Ex. 32).

Ex. 32

Harvey Grace pointed out that if the Rhapsody has been
written 'in 1903 instead of 1913 [*sic*], the F would have been
natural', this being the 'simplest possible example of folksong influence on harmony, the progression as written being
modal'.[4] At the outset, Butterworth portrays a scene of pastoral, elegiac wistfulness with carefully conceived orchestration
and dynamic shading, an effect which evidently influenced
E. J. Moeran in his *First Rhapsody* (1922), the opening bars of

[4] *Loc. cit.*, p. 61.

which are similar in mood, harmony and orchestration.[5] The
same instruments develop this opening phrase (*a*), by means
of imitation and sequence. Then follows the first quotation
from 'Loveliest of trees' (at the words in the song 'And stands
about the woodland ride'), scored here for solo clarinet (*b*);
this leads straight into the opening phrase of the vocal line of
the song (*c*), all in E major, the tonality of the song
(Ex. 33).[6]

Ex. 33

An unaccompanied cor anglais restates (*b*) in the same key, its
final note being the enharmonic mediant of a B flat minor
chord on lower strings, which reintroduces the opening bars
of the work a semitone higher, and with fuller scoring.

The music moves into E flat major and develops themes
already heard, in addition to quoting other ideas from the
accompaniment and the vocal line in 'Loveliest of trees'
(Ex. 34). Theme (*d*) combines vocal and instrumental motifs
(at 'wearing white for Eastertide'), while theme (*e*), scored
for brass, is derived from the piano interlude between the
first two verses. The music now grows more intense, with
fuller scoring, but soon quietens down to introduce a new
idea, in B minor, in the strings (Ex. 35).

[5] Geoffrey Self, *The Music of E. J. Moeran*, Toccata Press, London, 1986,
p. 36. Moeran was an admirer of Butterworth's music.

[6] *Cf* also Ex. 16 on p. 58.

Ex. 34

Ex. 35

Woodwind join in, and the music quickly builds up to a passionate climax, all the while developing theme (*f*). Michael Kennedy compares this climax to a passage in the finale of Vaughan Williams' *Pastoral Symphony*, where strings and woodwind have a dramatically intense dialogue, and he suggests these bars might almost be Butterworth's memorial.[7]

It is this climax that Butterworth, for the only time, uses all his resources; at its height, he brings back (*c*), played by

[7] *The Works of Ralph Vaughan Williams*, Oxford University Press, Oxford and London, 1964 (paperback edn. 1971, 2nd edn. 1980), p. 171.

trumpets. From now on, earlier themes are developed in new ways and with colourful orchestration; (*b*) and (*e*) assume further significance, the harp becomes more prominent, and there is even a very brief passage for bass clarinet, accompanied solely by three-part double-basses. These bars herald the coda, in A minor, which is basically a restatement of the opening bars. Theme (*a*) has not been much in evidence, but it does appear on a solo horn (in F minor) shortly before the coda, and is referred to by a solo viola some dozen bars before that, in A flat minor. In the coda clarinets and violas reverse roles, and, as a final masterstroke, Butterworth quotes the opening of the last song of the *Bredon Hill* cycle, 'With rue my heart is laden, for golden friends I had', on a solo flute (Ex. 36), before strings fade away on the final A minor chord. As Sir Thomas Armstrong has pointed out, this quotation 'is significant, and in view of what was soon to happen, almost prophetic'.[8]

Ex. 36

Of Butterworth's three surviving orchestral works, only the Rhapsody has no direct connection with folksong, yet the origins of his style are all too clearly derived from the traditional music of his native land. His absolute mastery of the orchestra is a most important feature of the Rhapsody, and owes little to Teutonic influences, although Armstrong finds the scoring similar to Mendelssohn's in its 'clarity and precision'.[9] The development of the middle section, leading up to the central climax, possibly owes something to Tchaikovsky,

[8] Introduction to the miniature score, Eulenburg, London, 1981.

[9] *Ibid.*

with its impassioned feeling of surging forward, but influences from abroad are generally negligible.

The Rhapsody received its premiere on 2 October 1913, during the Leeds Festival,[10] where it was played by the London Symphony Orchestra under Arthur Nikisch. Many prominent musicians were present, including Hugh Allen, Henry Colles, Henry Hadow, Cyril Rootham, Edward Dent and Vaughan Williams. Elgar, too, may have attended this performance, as his *Falstaff* was first heard that evening in Leeds. The festival music on 2 October included Verdi's *Requiem* in the morning, followed after lunch by the Rhapsody, Bach's *Jesu, meine Freude*, and Beethoven's Seventh Symphony, the concert eventually ending at 3.30 p.m.

The new work was most favourably received by critics and audience alike. Sir Adrian Boult recalled the final rehearsal in Leeds Town Hall, when he sat next to the composer:

> Nikisch, having finished the run-through, asked for his criticisms. George shook his head and thanked him: the performance had been exactly as he wished. Then he said quickly to me, 'You know, at the first rehearsal in London last week there were half-a-dozen small points I told him about. I was surprised that he didn't try any of them at the time, but he has remembered everything I said. I think that's pretty good'. That was indeed praise from one who was as critical of everyone (including himself). The performance, of course, made a deep impression.[11]

Butterworth's work was highly praised by some of England's leading musicians. Hadow later referred to the 'new voice that had come into English music',[12] Rootham to the

---

[10] Butterworth had attended the previous Leeds Festival, in October 1910, to hear the first performance of Vaughan Williams' *A Sea Symphony*.

[11] *Boult on Music*, Toccata Press, London, 1983, p. 32; this passage is from a brief reminiscence of the composer, and originally appeared as the Foreword to the 1948 reissue of the *Memorial Volume*.

[12] Letter to Sir Alexander, 19 June 1917, on receiving a score of the Rhapsody; *Scrapbook*, f. 54.

Sir Adrian Boult (courtesy of the Royal College of Music)

Rhapsody's 'remarkable qualities and first-rate workmanship',[13] while Dent expounded at some length on the work's
qualities and those of its composer:

> For some years back, I had become convinced that Vaughan
> Williams was our one really great composer [...] and, after
> the Leeds Festival of 1913, I had no doubt that George was the
> only younger man who could be placed alongside of him. The
> Rhapsody was a most beautiful piece of work, perfectly
> finished in technique, so clearly designed, so certain and so
> masterly in its execution, and so full of wonderful beauty and
> poetry [...].[14]

The Leeds performance was evidently of a high quality,
and praise was given to Nikisch's sympathetic reading of the
score. Although it was a 'happy day for George's friends, and
a great event in [his] career',[15] 'it was difficult to persuade
him that the applause required his presence on the plat-
form'.[16]

The critics were almost unanimous in regarding the
Rhapsody as a fine artistic achievement, and they praised its
orchestral colouring, the logical development of its musical
ideas, the portrayal of its wistful atmosphere, and so on. Two
or three unenlightened critics from the provinces had little
to commend, but the majority felt, as did Hadow, that a new
voice in English music had appeared, and showed enormous
promise.

Other conductors and orchestras soon included the
Rhapsody in their repertoire. London first heard it on 20
March 1914, at the Queen's Hall, Geoffrey Toye conducting
the Queen's Hall Orchestra in one of Bevis Ellis' concerts of
'Modern Orchestral Music'. This concert also included the

---

[13] Letter to Sir Alexander, 20 June 1917, also on receiving a score; *Scrapbook*, f. 56. Rootham was keen to perform the Rhapsody in Cambridge.

[14] Letter to Sir Alexander, 14 September 1916; *Scrapbook*, f. 63.

[15] Written by an 'Oxford friend' in *Oxford Magazine*, Extra No., 10 November 1916.

[16] Lennard's appreciation in *Memorial Volume*, p. 100.

London premiere of *The Banks of Green Willow,* three weeks after its first performance in Cheshire.

Toye (1889–1942) was a young English conductor occupied mainly in the opera house and theatre, and whose first appearance at the Queen's Hall this was; he had earlier collected and arranged songs for Mary Neal, and was the composer of the ballet *The Haunted Ballroom,* of which the waltz is often played separately. Ellis, of similar age, was active in promoting three concerts within eight days in March 1914, two orchestral concerts at the Queen's Hall, and a chamber concert at the Aeolian Hall. An Oxford graduate and another war victim, Ellis belonged to the de Walden family, who were patrons of the arts, and he had many friends in musical circles; a music library at Oxford was founded in his memory. Butterworth was a very close friend of his, as was Arnold Bax, who assisted Ellis in organising these concerts. The programme of 20 March comprised Bax's *Festival Overture,* the two Butterworth works, Dvořák's *The Noonday Witch,* Bax's *Four Orchestral Sketches* in their first complete performance and, after an interval, songs by Franck and Strauss, and Strauss' *Don Quixote,* conducted by Ellis himself.[17] Bax and Butterworth, apart from being colleagues of Ellis, had little in common musically; Bax certainly decried the nationalist school, although he saw in Vaughan Williams a 'composer of genius', and had little praise for Cecil Sharp, at whose Hampstead Conservatoire he had studied for a while.[18]

The second orchestral concert promoted by Ellis, and conducted by Toye, was held on 27 March; the important premiere given then was that of Vaughan Williams' *A London*

---

[17] In Bax's words, Ellis 'idolized Strauss, and I was told with bated breath by George Butterworth that I had the signal honour to be the only member of Ellis' circle allowed to make the least adverse criticism of his deity!' (*Farewell, My Youth,* Longmans, Green & Co., London, 1943, p. 93; 2nd revised edn. (including other writings by Arnold Bax, ed. Lewis Foreman), Scolar Press, Aldershot, 1992).

[18] *Ibid.,* pp. 16–17.

Symphony, a work which had close associations with Butter-worth. This concert also included the London premiere of Delius' *In a Summer Garden.*

During the latter part of the War, and after it, many other performances of the Rhapsody were given, including those by Landon Ronald (Manchester, 28 February 1917; Royal Albert Hall, 17 February 1918; Birmingham, 6 April 1921), Sir Henry Wood (Queen's Hall, 6 September 1917, 20 January 1918 and 19 November 1918; Nottingham, March 1920),[19] Adrian Boult (Queen's Hall, 4 March 1918; People's Palace, Mile End Road, 16 October 1921) and Eugene Goossens (Liverpool, 30 November 1918); other performances were given at Bristol, Bournemouth, Sheffield, Bradford, and Edinburgh (in December 1919, the first Scottish perform-ance). The performance Wood gave in 1917,[20] at a Promenade concert, caused the conductor to write to Sir Alexander in glowing terms and Sir Henry, indeed, became one of the work's champions. Generally, the Rhapsody was well received by audiences and critics at subsequent perform-ances – but there was now no speculatory hope of great things to come, as after the Leeds premiere, but rather a touching memorial of great things achieved. More than eighty years later, it remains one of the best-loved British orchestral works of the early part of this century.

The Banks of Green Willow

This orchestral piece dates from 1913, and is scored for a smaller orchestra than the Rhapsody, requiring only double woodwind and horns, trumpet, harp and strings, slightly fewer instruments, in fact, than in the *Two English Idylls*. As a third folksong idyll, *The Banks of Green Willow* has several points of contact with the earlier works: the length (it is shorter than the Rhapsody), the imaginative use of folksong

---

[19] Early in 1920, Frank Bridge deputised for Wood at very short notice, in a programme which included the Rhapsody, a work he barely knew, and, by all accounts, scored a notable success.

[20] It was billed, mistakenly, as the first London performance.

material, the arch-shaped structure, and the approximate
size of orchestra. Coming two or three years after the earlier
idylls, it generally shows a maturer command of orchestration
and compositional technique, and a richer sense of harmony,
all adding up to a work of contemplative beauty.

Butterworth described *The Banks of Green Willow* as a
'musical illustration to the folk-ballad of the same name'.[21] In
addition to this traditional tune, he uses another folk-song,
Green Bushes (first collected by Grainger in Lincolnshire in
1906), as well as an original theme. These three tunes supply
most of the thematic material. Butterworth himself collected
the title theme in June 1907 (Ex. 37(*a*)), but created a slightly
more flowing adaptation of the tune for use in this orchestral
idyll (Ex. 37(*b*)).

Ex. 37

(a)

(b)

A solo clarinet sets a pastoral scene with the title theme.

---

[21] Programme note to the first London performance, 20 March 1914,
reprinted in *Memorial Volume*, pp. 114–15.

Development follows in the strings, and flute and oboe begin to take a more active part. The mood changes with a $\frac{3}{2}$ *Maestoso* section, in which horns are prominent, and this leads directly to brief animated string writing (Ex. 38); this motif is developed into the central climax of the work, in which bars five and six from the opening theme are predominant.

Ex. 38

The music quickly quietens down, introducing *Green Bushes* on a solo oboe (Ex. 39(*a*)); Ex. 39(*b*) shows the tune as collected by Butterworth in July 1907, and transposed into A minor.

Ex. 39

(a)

Later, a solo flute takes over the tune in a passage which, accompanied by harp arpeggios, represents the epitome of English pastoral music. A slower passage, for strings alone, is followed in the closing bars by oboe and horn which recall the animated section, but now in a much calmer atmosphere.

(b)

The first performance of *The Banks of Green Willow* took place on 27 February 1914, when Adrian Boult conducted a combined orchestra of forty members of the Hallé and Liverpool Philharmonic, led by Arthur Catterall (of the Hallé).[22] The venue was the Public Hall, West Kirby, Cheshire, at first sight an unlikely place for a Butterworth – or, indeed, any – premiere, until one realises that Boult's parents lived in this town on the Wirral peninsula. This was the young conductor's first concert with a professional orchestra, and his varied programme also included a *Brandenburg* Concerto, arias by Mozart and Verdi, part of Schumann's Piano Concerto, the *Siegfried Idyll*, Wolf's *Italian Serenade* and the *Don Giovanni* Overture.

Butterworth himself directed a performance in Oxford the next day, but no details are known. London first heard the idyll at one of Ellis' concerts, on 20 March 1914; this performance was apparently the last occasion on which Butterworth heard his own music.

Love Blows as the Wind Blows
The song-cycle *Love Blows as the Wind Blows* has been unjustly neglected since its composition in 1911/12, although more

[22] Catterall (1883–1943) later led the BBC Symphony Orchestra from 1930 to 1936. He was also leader of his own quartet for many years, and, as a soloist, gave the premiere of Delius' Violin Sonata No. 1 in 1915, and of Moeran's Violin Concerto in 1942.

performances have taken place in recent years. Butterworth here set four poems from *Echoes*, by W. E. Henley.[23] As in the case of Oscar Wilde (and *Requiescat*), Henley, too, was capable of writing short, lyrical, wistful poems, which appealed to Butterworth, and settings of poems from *Echoes* appeared in the early years of this century from other English composers, including Delius, Gurney and Quilter. Butterworth's cycle is composed for medium voice and string quartet (or piano); Vaughan Williams may have made the piano arrangement. A revised version, for small orchestra, omitting one song and making several significant changes to the accompaniment and the vocal line, appeared in 1914. Neither version was published until 1921.

The use of a string quartet is interesting: Vaughan Williams had used this medium (with the addition of piano) a few years earlier, in his Housman cycle *On Wenlock Edge*, a work Butterworth much admired. In Butterworth's song-cycle, there is ample evidence of his sensitive use of instruments, which are never allowed to dominate the music, and of his rich, melodic gift, thoroughly absorbing both the folksong idiom and other compositional styles. In the revised, orchestral version, other composers occasionally spring to mind, and Butterworth's use of European influences is due, in part, to the nature of Henley's verse, in particular, its somewhat pessimistic *fin-de-siècle* atmosphere, and also to a slightly more advanced idiom, as a result of his close acquaintance with Vaughan Williams' *A London Symphony*, as well as a deeper knowledge of such composers as Wagner, Debussy and Elgar.

Some of the bare facts relating to the work seem to have

---

[23] William Ernest Henley (1849–1903) was a leading literary critic in his day and, with his huge physique, was the model for R. L. Stevenson's Long John Silver. His daughter, who died at four, became the inspiration for J. M. Barrie's Wendy in *Peter Pan*. For further information on Henley, *cf.* J. Wright, 'The Crippled Giant', *The Bedfordshire Magazine*, Vol. 2, No. 11, Winter 1949/50, pp. 115–16.

confused both Allen[24] and Michael Kennedy,[25] who refer to the accompaniment as being for 'piano and string quartet', and both again err in addition, surprisingly, à propos of the 1982 republication of the cycle, when it comes to naming the four songs. The titles are 'In the year that's come and gone'; 'Life in her creaking shoes' (or 'Love blows as the wind blows'); 'Fill a glass with golden wine' (omitted in the orchestral version); 'On the way to Kew' (or 'Coming up from Richmond').

'In the year that's come and gone'

There is a haunting atmosphere in this song, reminiscent of a few of the Housman settings and, indeed, of some of the orchestral music. The song is bound together by recurring themes and words, as two lovers reflect on the past year and look forward to the next. The minute, somewhat insignificant, introduction becomes the song-cycle's leitmotiv (Ex. 40), and the opening vocal phrase (Ex. 41) is never far away in this song; neither is the influence of Vaughan Williams, both in the vocal line and in the accompaniment, and there is more than a hint of the *Five Mystical Songs* (notably the third, 'Love bade me welcome'), a work contemporary with Butterworth's song-cycle.[26]

Ex. 40

There are frequent changes of tonality, and some modula-

---

[24] *Loc. cit.*

[25] Sleeve-note of EMI recording (ASD 3896).

[26] The *Five Mystical Songs* were first performed during the 1911 Three Choirs Festival (on 14 September) at Worcester; the soloist was Campbell McInnes.

Ex. 41

tions seem a little uneasy, but the 1914 revision improved a couple of weak moments, including the climactic point in the third verse (Ex. 42). The conclusion ('life's mysterious morrow') is particularly atmospheric with its quiet, undulating quavers (an important feature of this song) and the alternation of chords related to B major and G major.

Ex. 42

(a)   original vocal line

(b)   1914 revision

'Life in her creaking shoes'
('Love blows as the wind blows')
The mystery of love is compared to the vagaries of the wind (hence the subtitle, and the title of the cycle) and contrasted with the more formal and orderly ways of nature (stars, rivers, dews). This diversity is well reflected in Butterworth's setting, a rather staid and, in places, almost static accompaniment, contrasting with more passionate and dramatic music for the two love/wind references, which are much the same, apart from tonality. The revised version erased the odd superfluous

bar and changed the ending, so that there is a more convincing link with the fourth song (the third song being
omitted in the orchestral version). The leitmotiv occurs at
the words 'Love blows as the wind blows' both times, and also
appears at the conclusion of the original version, in the
accompaniment (Ex. 43).

Ex. 43

(a)

(b)

Some of the word-setting in this song and the delicacy of the
accompaniment suggest the idiom of Finzi's songs, which did
not begin to appear until some fifteen to twenty years later.

'Fill a glass with golden wine'
This song is less successful than any of the others, which may
well be the chief reason for Butterworth's omitting it in the
1914 revision. It is through-composed and firmly based in C
sharp minor, but neither the vocal line nor the accompaniment suggest he was particularly inspired when composing it.
No reference is made to the leitmotiv.

'On the way to Kew' ('Coming up from Richmond')
These reflections on times past by the River Thames are
provided with suitably haunting music, and this song, the

longest of the set, is certainly one of Butterworth's finest vocal settings. The opening accompaniment figure (Ex. 44 – the flowing river?) is present in some form throughout most of the song, breaking off only at 'And old, immortal words sang in my breast like birds', where there are subtle references to the leitmotiv (Ex. 45), and at the climax of the song, 'Not in vain, not in vain, Shall I look for you again'.

Ex. 44

Ex. 45

The accompaniment never dominates the music and acts as a perpetual background; subtle touches of word-painting and key shifts are evident here and there, and the atmospheric coda, including the leitmotiv again, brings to an end a group of songs that deserve to be far more widely known.

Early performances of *Love Blows as the Wind Blows* are not well documented, although it is known that on 3 June 1918 Frederic Grisewood and the English String Quartet (Frank Bridge's own ensemble – he played the viola in it – and one of the leading quartets in England at the time) performed three of the songs at the Royal College of Music ('Fill a glass with golden wine' was omitted). It is unlikely that many performances took place before 1921, the year of publication. Birmingham heard it that year (13 November) and the British Music Society[27] included it in a programme on 3 July 1922 at Seaford House, Belgrave Square, where it was not too warmly received.[28]

Fantasia **for orchestra**

Only sketches remain of the orchestral *Fantasia*. Its most likely date is 1914, since a Bayswater address is written on the score, and here Butterworth was living before war broke out. A short score is referred to in these sketches, but there is no trace of it. A hushed, dark-coloured opening, on bassoons and divided violas and cellos, leads to an *andantino* section in which one basic theme, first heard on oboe and violas (Ex. 46) is developed, but the score is too fragmentary for constructive comment. A *vivace* section of only a few bars includes a promising figure on trumpets, but there the music stops (Ex. 47).

The folksong idiom is readily apparent, but as in *Love Blows as the Wind Blows*, there are also changes in Butterworth's compositional style, with not a few influences from European

---

[27] Not the organisation which currently bears this name. The earlier society was started in June 1918 by Arthur Eaglefield Hull with Lord Howard de Walden (a poet and patron of the arts) as president, Hugh Allen as chairman, and a committee including Dent, Boult, Walford Davies and Geoffrey Toye; in spite of considerable support and success in the 1920s, it was disbanded in 1933.

[28] *Scrapbook*, ff. 513–17.

Ex. 46

Ex. 47

composers; and it was almost inevitable that Vaughan Williams' *A London Symphony*, a work with which Butterworth became very familiar,[29] should have some influence on any orchestral writing undertaken by Butterworth at this time. The *Fantasia* is scored for a large orchestra, including triple woodwind.

---

[29] *Cf.* pp. 120–22 and 169–171.

VI

BUTTERWORTH AND VAUGHAN WILLIAMS

During the last ten years of Butterworth's life, he maintained a close friendship with Vaughan Williams; had he survived the War, the friendship would doubtless have been as important and enduring as that between Vaughan Williams and Holst.

The year 1906 was a major turning-point in Butterworth's life, not least through the exciting discovery of English folk-song and folk-dancing, to which he was introduced by Vaughan Williams. This the elder composer called 'not an inhibiting, but a liberating influence; it certainly helped Butterworth to realize himself and to cast off the fetters of Teutonism'.[1] Elsewhere, Vaughan Williams refers to the influence Schumann and Brahms had on Butterworth's early works and to the 'Oxford manner' in music – 'that fear of self-expression which seems to be fostered by academic traditions'.[2]

Both composers were intensely interested in each other's compositions and in their general development as composers (although the amicable discussions did not quite extend to the legendary Vaughan Williams-Holst 'field days', during

---

[1] 'Chapter of Musical Autobiography', in Hubert Foss, *Ralph Vaughan Williams: A Study*, Harrap, London, 1950, p. 37; reprinted in (a) Ralph Vaughan Williams, *Some Thoughts on Beethoven's Choral Symphony, with Writings on Other Musical Subjects*, Oxford University Press, 1953, p. 156, (b) Ralph Vaughan Williams, *National Music and Other Essays*, p. 193.

[2] *Memorial Volume*, p. 94.

which they studied and criticised each other's works). Two
successive Leeds Festivals, in 1910 and 1913, brought each
composer's name to closer attention, Vaughan Williams with
A Sea Symphony (first performed on 12 October 1910, his 38th
birthday), and Butterworth with *A Shropshire Lad* Rhapsody
(2 October 1913). Each composer was at Leeds to hear the
other's work.

In the summer of 1912, a group of young musicians,
including Butterworth, formed a choral group to specialise in
early music. The choir was known as the Palestrina Society,
and Vaughan Williams was asked to be their conductor.
Choir and conductor explored what was then the relatively
unfamiliar territory of sixteenth-century music, as well as
works and folksong arrangements by Vaughan Williams
himself.[3] Butterworth's contemporary, Rebecca Clarke
(1886–1979), the composer and viola-player, was also a member of the choir.

It was Butterworth who first suggested to Vaughan
Williams, around 1911, the idea of a purely orchestral sym-
phony, and the elder composer related how much he owed to
Butterworth in the writing of *A London Symphony*.

> He had been sitting with us one evening, talking, smoking
> and playing [. . .] and, at the end of the evening, just as he was
> getting up to go, he said, in his characteristically abrupt way:
> 'You know, you ought to write a symphony'. I answered, if I
> remember aright, that I never had written a symphony, and
> never intended to. (This was not strictly true, for I had in
> earlier years sketched three movements of one symphony and
> the first movement of another, all now happily lost.) I suppose
> that Butterworth's words stung me and, anyhow, I looked out
> some sketches I had made for what, I believe, was going to
> have been a symphonic poem (!) about London, and decided
> to throw it into symphonic form. I showed the sketches to
> George, bit by bit as they were finished, and it was then that I
> realized that he possessed, in common with very few com-
> posers, a wonderful power of criticism of other men's work
> and insight into their ideas and motives. I can never feel too

[3] *Cf.* Ursula Vaughan Williams, *op. cit.*, p. 105.

grateful to him for all he did for me over this work and his help did not stop short at criticism.[4]

The Symphony was first performed a week later than the London premieres of *A Shropshire Lad* Rhapsody and *The Banks of Green Willow*, on 27 March 1914. The concert was again promoted by Bevis Ellis, and again conducted by Geoffrey Toye and Ellis himself, the programme also including music by Delius, Bax, Balakirev, Ravel and Franck. Vaughan Williams later wrote:

> When Ellis suggested that my symphony should be produced at one of his concerts, I was away from home[5] and unable to revise the score myself, and George, together with Ellis and Francis Toye[6] undertook to revise it and make a 'short score' from the original – George himself undertook the last movement. There was a passage which troubled him very much, but I could never get him to say exactly what was wrong with it; all he would say was: 'It won't do at all'. After the performance he at once wrote to tell me he had changed his mind. He wrote: 'A work cannot be a fine one until it is finely played, and it is still possible that ——— may turn out equally well. I really advise you not to alter a note of the symphony until after its second performance. The passages I kicked at didn't bother me at all, because the music as a whole is so definite that a little occasional meandering is pleasant rather than otherwise. As to the scoring, I frankly don't understand how it comes off so well, but it does all sound right, so there's nothing more to be said'.[7]

Butterworth, clearly, was very much attached to the Symphony and, at the instigation of Henry Colles, his former colleague on *The Times*, he wrote a brief article on the work

[4] Partly from *Memorial Volume*, pp. 92–93, partly from Foss, *op. cit.*, p. 37.

[5] He was staying in the Italian Riviera for part of the winter of 1913–14.

[6] Francis Toye (1883–1964), the brother of Geoffrey Toye, was, for many years, well-known as a critic and writer on music. He was also a supporter of Mary Neal's Espérance movement.

[7] *Memorial Volume*, p. 93.

for the *RCM Magazine*, which Colles was then editing.[8] Nobody was better suited to write this article, and Butterworth's complete understanding of the work's merits is much in evidence. It is a worthy, though short, introduction to Vaughan Williams' work as a whole. Butterworth also wrote the programme notes for the first performance, providing further insights into the work.

Immediately before the First World War began, Butterworth realised that the score of the Symphony might be lost for ever, since it was in Germany, either at Breitkopf und Härtel, the Leipzig publishing firm, or, as the composer told Michael Kennedy, with Fritz Busch, the conductor, to whom Tovey had suggested the score should be sent.[9] Butterworth, therefore, set about copying the full score from the orchestral parts which, fortunately, were still in London. He was helped by certain friends in this task, including Edward Dent, who was responsible for the first movement, Geoffrey Toye and the composer. Butterworth worked on one movement himself. When the score was printed after the War, Vaughan Williams dedicated the revised version of the work (1920) to Butterworth's memory.

The two composers doubtless saw much of each other between 1910 and the autumn of 1914, both living in close proximity in Chelsea. In July 1914, they were both in Oxford, at Hugh Allen's house, playing and 'singing' Vaughan William's recent opera, *Hugh the Drover*.[10]

---

[8] 'Vaughan Williams's *London Symphony*', *RCM Magazine*, Vol. 10, No. 2, Easter Term 1914, pp. 44–46; *cf.* also Appendix Five, pp. 169–71.

[9] Boult preferred the former suggestion, thinking the score was sent to Germany to be engraved. In the event, it was lost for ever; *cf. Boult on Music*, pp. 65–72, originally a radio talk given in July 1965. The reconstructed score is in the British Library, London (Add. MSS 51317 A-D).

[10] An anecdote concerning this event was told by Henry Ley (organist of Christ Church, Oxford) and is quoted in Ursula Vaughan Williams, *op. cit.*, p. 421.

Nobody mourned Butterworth's death in August 1916 more deeply than Vaughan Williams, who wrote to Holst from France, some time in the autumn of that year:

> I sometimes dread coming back to normal life with so many gaps – especially of course George Butterworth – he has left most of his MS to me – and now I hear that Ellis is killed – out of those 7 who joined up together in August 1914, only 3 are left.[11]

The exchange of letters between Vaughan Williams and Holst is fascinating, and one can only wonder if a similar collection between Vaughan Williams and Butterworth might have existed, had Butterworth lived longer. Sadly, no such letters survive.

Shortly after Butterworth's death, Vaughan Williams wrote to Sir Alexander about the publication of his son's music:

> one would like to publish the whole of that all too small list as a permanent memorial to him [...]. If a selection is to be made, I should suggest the *Shropshire Lad* Rhapsody, *The Banks of Green Willow*, and the beautiful Henley songs.[12]

He was keen to be responsible for checking Butterworth's manuscripts before they were published but, as he was serving abroad during the War, he felt this might be a problem if early publication were required. He cited Allen as the only other musician capable of doing this work.

In another letter to Sir Alexander, dated 16 August,[13] Vaughan Williams continued to express his admiration for the younger composer:

[11] Ursula Vaughan Williams and Imogen Holst (eds.), *Heirs and Rebels: Letters Written to Each Other and Occasional Writings on Music by Ralph Vaughan Williams and Gustav Holst*, Oxford University Press, 1959, p. 45.

[12] *Scrapbook*, ff. 48–49. Vaughan Williams was casual in dating letters; this one is merely headed 'Monday, September'. He believed *The Banks of Green Willow* to be Butterworth's finest orchestral work.

[13] Presumably 1916; *Scrapbook*, f. 60.

I think I know of no composer whose music expressed his character more exactly [. . .]. [He had] the determination to be and to say exactly what he meant and no other.

He goes on to speak of the music Butterworth did write and of 'that still bigger music which was still unfulfilled in him one cannot believe is lost – it *must* have its influence on the world somehow'.

Vaughan Williams' first wife, Adeline, also wrote to Butterworth's father, again reflecting the close relationship between the two musicians:

[Ralph] had George to turn to about his work, and was always so happy when he had written something that he liked and then in all that Ralph did was the thought how much further his work be carried on, and he looked so confidently to what George would do.[14]

---

[14] 15 August 1916 (?); *Scrapbook*, f. 104.

VII

EPILOGUE

The outbreak of war in August 1914 marked another turning-point, and the final phase, in Butterworth's short life; from this time until shortly before his death, he kept a diary, giving a detailed account of his remarkable military career.[1]

When war broke out, Butterworth was at Stratford, involved in one of Sharp's summer schools of folk-dancing. The school continued to run during the first days of the War, Butterworth writing to his future stepmother, Dorothea Mavor, on 7 August: 'There will be plenty of time to think about volunteering after the first enthusiasms have cooled down'.[2] The excitement of the times affected him none-theless, and it pleased him to learn of Dorothea escaping from Germany by car, immediately before the outbreak of war (she had been visiting a spa at Nauheim, near Wies-baden).

Within two weeks Butterworth was offered a commission by a friend of Sir Alexander but declined it, writing to his father on 19 August, 'it would be the wrong thing to take advantage of private influence at the present time'.[3] Butterworth returned to London from Stratford on 29 August and learned that some of his colleagues, including R. O. Morris,

---

[1] Butterworth's War Diary and letters home form a large proportion of the *Memorial Volume*, pp. 15–80, and are quoted extensively in Ian Copley's centennial tribute, *op. cit.*, pp. 16–51.

[2] *Memorial Volume*, p. 16.

[3] *Ibid.*, p. 16.

had been advised to join the Duke of Cornwall's Light Infantry; three days later, he and several musical and/or Oxford friends, including Bevis Ellis and Morris, enlisted as privates in this regiment. The following day they were drafted, along with several hundred other recruits, to Bodmin in Cornwall. Butterworth recorded the adverse conditions awaiting them there, concluding that, all in all, he found it a 'remarkable experience, the most surprising thing about it being the complete absence of any attempt at discipline'.[4]

Butterworth and his immediate circle now numbered eight men: 'P. A. Brown, University Teacher [and graduate of New College, Oxford], G. Butterworth, F. B. Ellis, Musician, R. A. Ellis, Engineer and Farmer [brother of F. B. Ellis], F. H. Keeling, Journalist, R. O. Morris, Musician, E. G. Toye, Musician [a last-minute recruit] and R. C. Woodhead, Civil Servant'.[5] On 4 September, they – and about five hundred others – were transferred to Aldershot to undergo a period of basic training. Here they found a shortage of officers and NCOs, and soon Keeling and Woodhead became lance-corporals. Applications for commissions were invited, and Toye's was accepted.

> The rest of us, after much consultation, decided that the most important thing for us was to keep our party intact; having arranged to serve together, it would obviously be unfair on those who might be left if some of us became officers [Toye was an exception, as he joined at the eleventh hour] – so we told the Major [Barnet] that unless all could have commissions, we would continue as we were; naturally enough, that was considered as equivalent to a refusal.[6]

Conditions at Aldershot were far from ideal; tents were overcrowded, canteens ill-equipped, and there was a distinct lack of protective clothing. Butterworth was one of the relatively few men wealthy enough to able to buy the clothing

[4] *Ibid.*, p. 20.

[5] *Ibid.*, p. 22.

[6] *Ibid.*, pp. 25–26.

that was required, as well as extra meals in nearby Farnborough.

On 24 September, he was to write:

> The question of commissions has again cropped up; we have all been wavering in our minds about it for some time, and seeing crowds of beardless youths shipped down here as officers has made us rather less satisfied with our position as privates [...]. Within the last few days several of us have been approached [...] on the subject of commissions. Only yesterday I had a letter from General Ovens, of the North Command, practically offering me a commission in his Brigade, the 68th, stationed at Pirbright, near here; and also asking me to name others of our party.[7]

Butterworth decided to follow up this offer, and proposed the names of the six remaining members of his group in pairs – the Ellis brothers, Brown and Woodhead, Morris and himself. Early in October, the offer of commissions for the six men arrived, and eventually they were transferred to Bullswater Camp, General Ovens' headquarters at Woking. Here there were further delays; 'In any case it was necessary for us all to go up to London to get uniform and kit, and so it was decided that we were to remain at home until sent for'.[8] That meant several days, which Butterworth found very annoying: 'After five strenuous weeks, the feeling of being absolutely idle, while everyone else was busy, was trying in the extreme'.[9] By the second week in October, they were back at Bullswater Camp, disposed as follows: the Ellis brothers as first lieutenants in the 10th Northumberland Fusiliers, Woodhead as first lieutenant in the 12th Durham Light Infantry, and Brown, Morris and Butterworth as second lieutenants in the 13th Durham Light Infantry. They were all originally appointed first lieutenants, but 'as the 13th Durhams seemed

7 *Ibid.*, pp. 33–34.

8 *Ibid.*, p. 40.

9 *Ibid.*, p. 40.

to be particularly strong in junior officers, Brown, Morris and self requested to be made seconds'.[10]

Butterworth now found himself commanding a platoon in 'C' Company, and he seems to have enjoyed his new position of authority, especially as most of those under him were Durham miners, men with whom he got on particularly well. The winter of 1914/15 was spent in barracks at Aldershot, and in the spring of 1915 there was a move to Bramshott, near Liphook in Hampshire, where he was promoted to full lieutenant, and, for nearly a month, was an Acting Company Commander, 'in charge of 240 men, scarcely one of whom I know by sight!'[11]

Life in army camp or barracks seemed very monotonous at times, and both Butterworth and his men were keen to see active service. Their wish was granted in August 1915, when orders came that they were to mobilise, and on the 25th the Brigade moved to France.

In the first week or so, military training resumed its dull and monotonous routine; there was little evidence of war and scarcely any information about what they were supposed to be doing. One of Butterworth's daily tasks was the 'censoring of men's letters', which he found to be 'of great human interest. I don't think I ever before realised the difference between married and single!'[12] During 6 and 7 September, the Brigade marched another 35 miles to within five or six miles of the front, close to Armentières, and, at last, on the following day, they received clearer instructions as to their duties:

> We were to go up into the trenches by platoons, for 'instructional purposes', 24 hours at a stretch, being attached to the units actually on duty there. We were to do this for four days (two days in and two out), and then retire in safety for further

---

[10] *Ibid.*, p. 41.

[11] *Ibid.*, p. 48.

[12] *Ibid.*, p. 52.

training and finally take up our own positions in the line, in perhaps two or three weeks' time [...].[13]

By 11 September, Butterworth had recorded his first 24 hours in the trenches and his first real experience of the War, but after nine days had passed, he was to write of having so far seen 'only one shell burst' and having not seen 'a single (a) dead man, (b) wounded man, (c) German, (d) gun'.[14] Life was now divided into short periods in the trenches and a similar time resting; he was able to write lengthy letters home, but he became somewhat anxious over the amount of information he included in them. In November, military action seemed limited: 'We have now had a full fortnight's "rest", and for myself it has been almost literally rest. I have done practically nothing but eat, sleep and play chess! [...] There is nothing else to do here – no places to go, the most frightfully dull country imaginable, and any amount of rain'.[15]

On 4 November, his colleague P. A. Brown was killed in action near La Houssoie. (Apart from Butterworth himself, one other member of the circle lost his life in the war – Bevis Ellis at Combles, in September 1916.)

Early in 1916, Butterworth was granted leave for a week, to attend his father's wedding to Dorothea Mavor on 26 January, and then spent most of February on a signalling course at Hazebrucke. He enjoyed this new experience, not least because he could get away from what had been until then a fairly monotonous existence, and he wrote at the end of February: 'it is the first time I have ever taken the slightest interest in anything scientific, and I am beginning to feel quite a practical man'.[16] His battalion now began to move south in stages towards the Somme, arriving there in July, during which month it was heavily involved in the conflict.

---

[13] *Ibid.*, p. 53.

[14] *Ibid.*, p. 57.

[15] *Ibid.*, p. 63.

[16] *Ibid.*, p. 68.

Butterworth's Military Cross (from the Butterworth Memorial Volume)

Butterworth soon found himself in charge of his company, after the wounding of the Officer Commanding, and he remained in this position of authority until his death. He was recommended for the Military Cross, 'for conspicuous gallantry in action' at Bailiff Wood (9 July), and recommended for – and awarded – the Military Cross 'for commanding his company with great ability and coolness' at Pozières (17–19 July).[17] No mention was made of this honour in his letters home.

On 1 August, the Brigade was sent to the front for the final time, and it was at around this date that the trench that was later named after Butterworth was dug, three days before a successful attack on Munster Alley, another trench running between the German and English lines. It was here that Butterworth met his death at about 4.45 a.m. on 5 August. Brigadier-General H. Page Croft, commander of the 68th Infantry Brigade, later wrote to Sir Alexander of the composer's final moments:

> I went up to the farthest point reached with Lieut. Kaye-Butterworth. The trench was very low and broken, and he kept urging me to keep low down. I had only reached the Battalion Headquarters on my return when I heard poor Butterworth, a brilliant musician in times of peace and an equally brilliant soldier in times of stress, was shot dead by a bullet through the head. So he, who had been so thoughtful for my safety, had suffered the same fate he had warned me against only a minute before.[18]

Butterworth's body could not be brought out to be buried near the Regimental Aid-post, since he was killed so near to the enemy line, and so he and a colleague were buried close to Munster Alley, the grave being marked with his name and

---

[17] Letter to Sir Alexander from Lt. Col. H. Wilkinson, *Scrapbook*, f. 11. It continues: 'By his energy and total disregard of personal safety, he got his men to accomplish a good piece of work in linking up the front line.' Butterworth was again awarded the Military Cross on the night of his death.

[18] *Memorial Volume*, p. 80.

The Thiepval Memorial
(courtesy of M. E. A. Hardwidge and John Dodd)

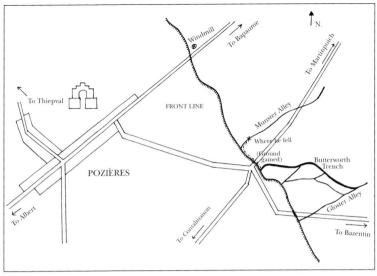

*Map showing the location of Butterworth's trench
(drawn by M. E. A. Hardwidge)*

regiment. No trace of Butterworth's grave remains, but his name does appear on the Thiepval memorial nearby.

During his military career, Butterworth, on many occasions, showed remarkable qualities as a leader of men, and with his unassuming, unselfish yet courageous attitude, gained the respect of all who served under him. He was especially popular with the Durham miners under his command and even collected songs from them. Temperamentally he was a northerner, and the independence and forthright nature of people from Yorkshire and Durham particularly appealed to him. But few realised his musical talents and reputation, as exemplified by General Ovens who, on writing to Sir Alexander, praised Butterworth's ability as a soldier but commented: 'I did not know he was so very distinguished in music'.[19]

No reference to musical matters is made at all in the War Diary and letters home, and one can only assume that the

[19] *Ibid.*, p. 84.

summer of 1914 marked the end of his brief musical career. Before he went to France, Butterworth destroyed that part of his output he deemed unworthy – mainly piano pieces and songs – so that the full extent of his work may never be known. Nevertheless, what has survived contains enduring qualities of exquisite workmanship and musicality, with never a note too many.[20] Always a seeker for beauty in whatever he composed, Butterworth largely avoided the influences of such pre-War 'modernists' as Strauss and Debussy, in favour of preserving something of the folksong heritage of his native land – although in some of the later works (*Fantasia, Love Blows as the Wind Blows*, 'On the idle hill of summer'), there are definite hints of European mainstream composers (chiefly Wagner and Tchaikovsky) and of Elgar, suggesting that the folksong influence was less relevant for his purpose here, and, indeed, implying a change of direction in his musical language. The influence of Vaughan Williams' *A London Symphony* on his compositional style cannot, of course, be ruled out.

In spite of his strong links with London – he lived in Chelsea between 1910 and 1914, as well as working, studying and securing performances in the capital – Butterworth was far more at home with country people, collecting folksongs, performing morris dances, playing cricket, and so on. Not for him London society, but rather the natural simplicity of rural life; it was, according to Lennard,

> right for *him* to relate his work as a composer to the elemental simplicities of folk music. I once seriously suggested to him that he should become a village inn-keeper, for I thought he would have enough leisure for composition and would find it easier to express himself fully and truly in music if he became really rooted in the country.[21]

---

[20] Such a small output of finely wrought works can be compared to that of Duparc.

[21] *George Butterworth – The Man and His Music*, BBC Home Service, 14 July 1942.

Whistler's commemorative window at Radley College
(courtesy of L. Whistler)

In all of Butterworth's output, the man and the music are inseparable. He was very much a man of the English country-side, as was Housman, whose verses so fired the composer's imagination. The culmination of this partnership was his masterpiece, the Rhapsody, *A Shropshire Lad*, described as an epilogue, but surely also a summary of his brief life's work. Butterworth was no innovatory composer, nor was his music very influential, but he will remain an important minor figure with a reputation based on a handful of works, the sincerity and musical value of which assure him a place in the history of English music.

Appendix One

CATALOGUE
OF BUTTERWORTH'S MUSIC

Works are listed in chronological order under the following headings: orchestral music, songs, choral music, chamber and instrumental music; his collections of folksongs and morris dances are listed in Appendix Two.[1] The following system has been used: title, date of composition, orchestration, location of manuscript, publisher and date of publication, details of the first performance and, where appropriate, of the first London performance.

I. ORCHESTRAL MUSIC

Barcarolle
Date: unknown.
Orchestration: unknown.
MS: lost (unpublished).
First performance: 2 April 1903, Eton College/School
                   orchestra/George Butterworth.

Two English Idylls
Date: 1. 1910–11 (at end of score, 1909/1911
                   is erased).
                   2. 1911.
Orchestration: 2 (+ piccolo)-2-2-2; 4-0-0-0; timpani,
                   triangle; harp; strings
MS: Bodleian Library, Oxford (MSS. Mus.

---

[1] *Cf.* pp. 144–163, below.

c.302–303).

Published: Stainer and Bell, 1920.
First performance: 8 February 1912, Oxford Town Hall/
                        Oxford University Musical Club
                        orchestra/Hugh Allen.
First London
  performance: 31 August 1919, Queen's Hall/New
                        Queen's Hall Orchestra/Sir Henry
                        Wood.

Rhapsody, *A Shropshire Lad*
(Originally Prelude: *The Land of Lost Content*, then Prelude: *The Cherry Tree*)

Date: 1911.
Orchestration: 2-2(+ cor anglais)-2(+ bass clarinet)-2;
                        4-2-3-1; timpani; harp; strings.
MS: Bodleian Library, Oxford (MSS. Mus.
                        c.304–306); piano score (MSS. Mus.
                        c.298, ff. 410).
Published: Novello, 1917; miniature score,
                        Eulenburg, 1981 (No. 1382).
First performance: 2 October 1913, Leeds Town Hall/
                        London Symphony Orchestra/Arthur
                        Nikisch.
First London
  performance: 20 March 1914, Queen's Hall/Queen's
                        Hall Orchestra/Geoffrey Toye.

The Banks of Green Willow
Date: 1913.
Orchestration: 2-2-2-2; 2-1-0-0; harp; strings.
MS: Bodleian Library, Oxford (MSS. Mus.
                        c.301).
Published: Stainer and Bell, 1919.
First performance: 27 February 1914, Public Hall, West
                        Kirby, Cheshire/players from the Hallé
                        and Liverpool Philharmonic Orchestras/
                        Adrian Boult.
First London
  performance: 20 March 1914, Queen's Hall/Queen's
                        Hall Orchestra/Geoffrey Toye.
Arrangements: (a) for clarinet and piano, by Robin de
                        Smet (Fentone, London, 1987)

(b) for piano, by John Mitchell (Thames Publishing, London, 1993).

Fantasia

Date: c.1914
Orchestration: 3-2(+ cor anglais)-2(+ bass clarinet)-2 (+ double bassoon); 4-2-3-1; strings.
MS: Bodleian Library, Oxford (MS. Mus. b.15, ff. 72–79). Unpublished and incomplete.

II. SONGS

Crown winter with green

Date: Unknown, but early.
Words: Robert Bridges.
MS: Lost (unpublished).
No performance details known.

Haste on, my joys!

Date: Unknown, but early.
Words: Robert Bridges.
MS: Lost (unpublished).
No performance details known.

I will make you brooches

Date: Unknown, but probably early.
Words: R. L. Stevenson.
MS: British Library, London (Add. MS. 54369).
Published: Augener, 1920; Stainer and Bell, 1974.
First performance: unknown.

I fear thy kisses

Date: 'VI-09' erased on title page of autograph score, but 1909 at the end.
Words: Shelley.
MSS: (a) Bodleian Library, Oxford (MSS. Mus. c.298, ff. 20–21); (b) British Library,

	London (Add. MS. 54369).
Published:	Augener, 1919; Stainer and Bell, 1974.
First performance:	unknown.

Six Songs from 'A Shropshire Lad'

Date:	1909–11.
Words:	A. E. Housman.
	(1. 'Loveliest of trees' (1910–11); 2. 'When I was one-and-twenty' (arranged); 3. 'Look not in my eyes'; 4. 'Think no more, lad'; 5. 'The lads in their hundreds'; 6. 'Is my team ploughing?'.)
MSS:	(a) Eton College Library; (b) British Library, London (Add. MS. 54369).
Published:	Augener, 1911; Stainer and Bell, 1974. 'Is my team ploughing?' also published (Augener) in a higher key.
Dedication:	'V. A. B. K.' (Victor Annesley Barrington-Kennett).
First performance:	(?) 16 May 1911, at a meeting of the Oxford University Musical Club/ Campbell McInnes (baritone)/George Butterworth (piano); 'The lads in their hundreds' was not performed, although Sir Adrian Boult wrote the words of the song in his copy of the programme.
First London performance:	20 June 1911, Aeolian Hall/J. Campbell McInnes (baritone)/Hamilton Harty (piano).

(Orchestrated by Lance Baker)

Orchestration:	2-2-2(+ bass clarinet)-2; 2-2-0-0; timpani; harp; strings.
MS:	Lance Baker (unpublished).
First performance (rehearsal only):	17 November 1965/Richard Edwards/ London Repertoire Orchestra/Ruth Gipps.

Bredon Hill and Other Songs

Date:	1909–11.
Words:	A. E. Housman.
	(1. 'Bredon Hill'; 2. 'Oh fair enough are

sky and plain' (1909); 3. 'When the lad for longing sighs' (1910); 4. 'On the idle hill of summer' (1911); 5. 'With rue my heart is laden' (1910).)

MSS:	(a) Eton College Library (except 'On the idle hill of summer'); (b) British Library, London (Add. MS. 54369).
Published:	Augener, 1912; Stainer and Bell, 1974; 'Bredon Hill' also published in a higher key (Augener, 1912).
First performance:	(?) 16 May 1911, at a meeting of the Oxford University Musical Club/ J. Campbell McInnes (baritone)/George Butterworth (piano); 'On the idle hill of summer' was not performed.

Requiescat

Date:	'III–1911' on title page of autograph score.
Words:	Oscar Wilde.
MSS:	(a) Bodleian Library, Oxford (MSS. Mus. c.298, ff. 24–25); (b) British Library, London (Add. MS. 54369).
Published:	Augener, 1920; Stainer and Bell, 1974; also published (Augener) in a higher key.
First performance:	unknown.

Love Blows as the Wind Blows, for medium voice and string quartet, or piano

Date:	1911–12
Words:	W. E. Henley. (1. 'In the year that's come and gone'; 2. 'Life in her creaking shoes' (or 'Love blows as the wind blows'); 3. 'Fill a glass with golden wine'; 4. 'On the way to Kew' (or 'Coming up from Richmond').)
MS:	Bodleian Library, Oxford (MSS. Mus. c.300).
Published:	Novello, 1921; Thames Publishing, 1982, for medium voice and piano.
First performance:	unknown.

Revised version: 1914 (with orchestra, and omitting the
                        third song)
Orchestration: 1-1-2-1; 1-0-0-0; strings (6-6-4-4-2).
MS: Bodleian Library, Oxford (MSS. Mus.
                        c.299)
Published: Novello, 1921.
First performance: unknown.

III. CHORAL MUSIC

Three hymn tunes
Date: c.1896–99.
Words: 1. 'My father, hear my prayer' (author
                        unidentified); 2. 'Hear Thy children,
                        gentle Jesus' (author unidentified);
                        3. (No words).
MS: Bodleian Library, Oxford (*Scrapbook*,
                        ff. 548– 50).

On Christmas Night
Date: 1912
Words: Traditional; arrangement of English
                        traditional carol for SATB
                        (unaccompanied).
MS: not located.
Published: Augener, 1912.
First performance: unknown.
(Butterworth noted this version of the tune in April 1907
from a Mr Knight, of Horsham, Sussex.)

We get up in the morn
Date: 1912
Words: Traditional; arrangement of English
                        traditional harvest-song for TTBB
                        (unaccompanied).
MS: not located.
Published: Arthur P. Schmidt, Boston, 1912;
                        Augener, 1935.
First performance: unknown.

In the Highlands
Date: 1912

Words:	R. L. Stevenson; three-part song for female voices (SSA) and piano.
MS:	Not located.
Published:	Arthur P. Schmidt, Boston, 1912; Augener, 1930.
First performance:	unknown.

IV. CHAMBER AND INSTRUMENTAL MUSIC

String Quartet

Date:	unknown, but before July 1904.
MS:	lost (unpublished).

No performance details known.

Sonata for Violin and Piano

Date:	unknown, but before July 1904.
MS:	lost (unpublished).

No performance details known.

Firle Beacon, for piano.

Date:	unknown, but before 1911.
MS:	lost (unpublished).

No performance details known.

Duo for Two Pianofortes: Rhapsody on English Folk Tunes

Date:	unknown.
MS:	lost (unpublished).
First performance:	26 June 1910, Eton College/George Butterworth and E. R. Speyer.

Suite, for string quartet

Date:	*c*.1910. (i) *Andante con moto, molto espressivo*; (ii) *Scherzando – non allegro*; (iii) *Allegro molto*; (iv) *Molto moderato ed espressivo*; (v) *Moderato*
MS:	Bodleian Library, Oxford (MSS. Mus. c.297). Unpublished.
First performance:	unknown.

Appendix Two

FOLKSONGS AND MORRIS DANCES COLLECTED BY BUTTERWORTH

The complete collection of Butterworth's Folk Music Manuscripts is to be found on microfilm in Cecil Sharp House, London. The songs and dances are systematically arranged in several volumes, beginning with three volumes of folk-dance tunes, including the Filkins and Bledington Morris tunes. These are followed by two volumes of the words of folksongs, several volumes of the tunes, including the Bucknell Morris tunes, morris dances, sword dances, transcriptions of Playford's *The English Dancing Master* and the *Diary of Morris Dance Hunting*. In all, Butterworth collected nearly 300 folksongs, 134 dances in field-notations, and 29 dance tunes arranged for piano.

I. BUTTERWORTH'S FOLK MUSIC MANUSCRIPTS

Volume 1 (folk dance tunes)
Hit and Miss, Heart's Ease, Peppers Black, The Bath, Saturday Night and Sunday Morning, Wallingford House, Duke of York's Delight, Nobody's Jig, Christchurch Bells, Young Jenny, Love lies a-bleeding, Westmoreland, Step Stately, Aye me or *The Simphony, The Whin, Roger of Coverly, Lilli Burlero, Juice of Barley, Maids Morris, Jenny come tie my cravat, Prince Rupert's March, Jack Pudding, A Health to Betty, Jog on, Put on thy smock on Monday, The Gossips Frolic, Mr Isaac's Magot, The Mock Hobby Horse, Jigg it E Foot, Scotch Cap, Maiden's blush, Orleans baffled, Every lad his lass, The Collier's Daughter, Up Goes Ely, The Mary and Dorothy, The Coronation Day, Lady Banbury's Hornpipe, The Punk's Delight, Kemp's Jig, The Pursuit, Frisky Jenny* or *The Tenth of June, Humours of the Barn, Cockle-shells, Albion Queen, Pool's Hole, King of Poland, Crossbey Square, Half Hannikin, Gunnie Pug, The fits come on me now, The Milk-maid's Bob, Under and over, Mill-field, Daphne, Drive the cold winter away, The*

maid peeped out of the window, The New Exchange, Woodicock, Greenwood, The Cherping of the Lark.

Volume 2 (folk dance tunes)
Filkins Morris Tunes ('given by John Pougher, Filkins, July 1912'):
Hey Diddle Dis, Princess Royal, Cuckoo's Nest ('approx.'), *Constant Billy, Highland Mary, Maid of the Mill, Old Woman Tossed Up, Bobby and Joan.*
Bledington tunes: *Trunkles* (given by Charles Benfield, 'aged 72'), *Ladies of Pleasure, William and Nancy, Lumps of Plum Pudding* (given by Ted Gibbs, 'aged 74').
Piano arrangements: *Trunkles, Ladies of Pleasure, Lumps of Plum Pudding, Bonny Green, The Queen's Delight, Saturday Night, Shepherd's Hey, William and Nancy.*

Volume 3 (folk dance tunes – all piano arrangements)
Upon a Summer's Day, Jack a Lent, Greenwood, Broome, the Bonny, Bonny Broome, Confess, If all the world were paper, Stingo, Row well ye mariners, Argeers, Spring Garden, Up tails all, Irish Trot, The Phoenix, Touch and Take, Irish Lady, Althea, Sweet Kate, Catching of Flees, Hunsdon House, Maiden Lane, Merry Conceit.

Volumes 4 and 5 (words of folksongs); Volumes 6a, 6b, 7a, 7b, 7c, 7d and 7e (folksong tunes). Volume 7d also includes Morris dances and sword dances:
Bucknell Morris Tunes (given by Will Rolfe, 1912) *Bonny Green, Queen's Delight, Bonnets so blue, Saturday night, Room for Cuckolds, Old Woman, Old Black Joe, Trunkles*; New Morris Dances: *Step and fetch her* (Bampton), *Country Gardens* (Longborough), *Banks of the Dee* (Field Town), *Staines Morris* (Longborough), *Gallant Hussar* (Longborough).
Volumes 8a, 8b and 9 (Playford's *The English Dancing Master*)
Volume 10 (*Diary of Morris Dance Hunting*).

II. FOLKSONG TUNES COLLECTED BY GEORGE BUTTERWORTH

Some of the folksongs Butterworth collected were published in his lifetime, and others have been edited in recent years by Michael Dawney; the majority remain in manuscript.
There are five published sources:
1. *Journal of the Folksong Society*, Vol. 4, No. 15, December 1910 (referred to in the following list as *JFSS* 15);

2. *Journal of the Folksong Society*, Vol. 4, No. 17, January 1913 (*JFSS* 17);
3. *Folk Music Journal*, Vol. 3, No. 2, 1976 (*FMJ*);
4. *The Ploughboy's Glory*, English Folk Dance and Song Society, London, 1977 (*PG*);
5. *Folk Songs from Sussex*, Augener, London, 1913; reprinted Stainer and Bell, London, 1974 (*FSS*).

There are two manuscript sources:
1. British Library, London (Add. MS. 54369);
2. Cecil Sharp House, London (*FSS*).

The complete list below is in chronological order and uses the following system: date, title, indication (where appropriate) of a joint collection with Francis Jekyll or Vaughan Williams ('+ FJ' or '+ VW'), name of singer and location, manuscript or published source.

Title	Joint Collection	Singer and Location Source	Published?
September 1906			
The basket of eggs	+ FJ	Mr Colcombe, Weobley, Herefordshire	MS
A brisk young sailor	+ FJ	Mr Colcombe	MS
Lord Bateman	+ FJ	Mr Colcombe	MS
William Taylor	+ FJ	Mr Colcombe	MS
Sweet primroses	+ FJ	Mr Colcombe	MS
September? 1906			
Erin's lovely home	+ FJ	Mr Fletcher, Credenhill, Herefordshire	MS
Lord Bateman		Mr William Atkins, Windmill Hill, Sussex	MS
October 1906			
The undaunted female		Unnamed singer, Abingdon, Berks. (now Oxon.)	MS
The bold fisherman		Unnamed singer, Headington, Oxon.	MS
February 1907			
Come my own one		Mr Chalcraft, Petworth, Sussex	MS
April 1907			
The Queen's health		Mr George Knight, Horsham, Sussex	*JFSS* 17, p. 294
The ploughboy's glory		Mr George Knight, Horsham, Sussex	*PG*, p. 33
Come all you little Irish girls		Mr George Knight	*JFSS* 17, p. 346
On Christmas night all Christians sing		Mr George Knight	MS
Phoebe and her dark-eyed sailor		Mr George Knight	MS

Title	Joint Collection	Singer and Location Source	Published?
The mistress's health		Mr George Knight	MS
The cruel father and affectionate lovers		Mr George Knight	MS
Come all you jolly ploughboys		Mr George Knight	MS
April 1907			
Now we've drunk our master's health		Mr George Knight	MS
Barbara Allen		Mr Morley, Wartling, Sussex	MS
Jolly fellows that follow the plough		Mr Ede, Bosham, Sussex	MS
Just as the tide was flowing		Mr Weeker, Ticehurst, 'Kent' (error for Sussex)	MS
Sweet primroses (The banks of)		Unnamed singer, Battle, Sussex	MS
The undaunted female		Unnamed singer, Battle, Sussex	MS
The ploughboy's glory		Mr Pocock, Flowers Green, Sussex	MS
Come all you jolly ploughboys		Mr Pocock	MS
May 1907			
Come all you little Irish girls		Mr Tom Anstey, Beckley, Oxon.	*JFSS* 17, p. 345
'Twas by the town of Weddingmore		Unnamed singer, Charlton-on-Otmoor, Oxon.	*JFSS* 17, p. 341

Song	Singer	Source
The saucy sailor boy[1]	Mr Henry Webb, Stanton St John, Oxon.	*JFSS* 17, p. 342
Barbara Allen	Mr Henry Webb	MS
Oxford city	Mr Henry Webb	MS
Sweet primroses	Mr Henry Webb	MS
Barbara Allen	Mr Jim Wharton, Stanton St John, Oxon.	MS
Bonny blue handkerchief	Mr Jim Wharton	MS
The murder of Maria Marten	Mr Jim Wharton	MS
The bonny bunch of roses, oh!	Mr Nappin, Stanton St John, Oxon.	MS
Fair maid walking down in the garden	Mr Nappin	MS
Green mossy banks of the Lea	Mr Nappin	MS
The Irish girl	Mr Nappin	MS
'Twas by the town of Weddingmore	Mr Nappin	MS
Jack and the game	Unnamed singer, Stanton St John, Oxon.	MS
'Twas by the town of Weddingmore	Mr Nixie, Oakley, 'Oxon.' (probably Bucks.)	MS
'Twas by the town of Weddingmore	Mr Thomas Gibbs, Brill, Buckinghamshire	MS
The bold fisherman	Mr Thomas Gibbs	MS

June 1907

Song	Singer	Source
You seamen bold ('words noted in Shropshire')	Mr Henry Akhurst, Lr. Beeding, Sussex	*JFSS* 17, p. 320

[1] *Cf.* 'Come my own one' in *Folk Songs from Sussex*.

Title	Joint Collection	Singer and Location Source	Published?
Henry Martin		Mr Henry Akhurst	MS
Salisbury Plain[2]		Mr Henry Akhurst	MS
Green bushes		Mr Ned Harding	*FMJ*, p. 107
'Twas of a brisk and lively lad		Mr Ned Harding	MS
The bold thresherman		Mr Ned Harding	MS
The banks of green willow		Mr & Mrs Cranstone, Billingshurst, Sussex	*PG*, p. 12; *FMJ*, p. 103
The bonny bunch of roses, oh!		Mr & Mrs Cranstone	MS
On Christmas night all Christians sing		Mr & Mrs Cranstone	MS
'Twas of a brisk and lively lad		Mr & Mrs Cranstone	MS
When righteous Joseph wedded was		Mrs Cranstone, Billingshurst	MS
Just as the tide was flowing		Mrs Cranstone	MS
Lord Bateman		Mrs Cranstone	MS
Seventeen come Sunday		Mrs Cranstone	*JFSS* 17; *FSS*, p. 18
Roving in the dew		Mrs Cranstone	*FSS*, p. 20
The trees they do grow high		Mr Cranstone	MS
The Irish girl		Mr Hoare, Houghton, Sussex	MS
The bonny bunch of roses, oh!		Mr Hoare	MS

[2] July 1907 in *JFSS* 17, p. 323.

Song	Source	Reference
Seventeen come Sunday	Mr Hoare	MS
The bonny bunch of roses, oh!	Mr Walter Searle, Amberley, Sussex	MS
The cruel father and affectionate lovers	Mr Walter Searle	MS
Come my own one	Children of Mr Walter Searle, Sussex	JFSS 17; FSS, p. 12
The bold thresherman	Mr Netley, Nutbourne, Sussex	MS
Henry Martin	Mr Sendal, The Crabtree, Lr. Beeding, Sussex	MS
Henry Martin	Mr Jack Feast, Lr. Beeding, Sussex	MS
Henry Martin	Mr Walter Birfield, Barns Green, Sussex	MS
Seventeen come Sunday	Mr Henry Webb, Stanton St John, Oxon.	MS
Just as the tide was flowing	Mr H. Bush, Stanton St John, Oxon.	MS

July 1907

Song	Source	Reference
You seamen bold	Mr Harwood	JFSS 17, p. 321
The ploughboy's glory	Mr Harwood	MS
Salisbury Plain	Mr Harwood	MS
Come all you jolly ploughboys	Mr Harwood	MS
You seamen bold	Mr George Dearling, W. Burton, Pulborough, Sussex	JFSS 17, p. 321
Green bushes	Mr George Dearling	FMJ, p. 108
Highland soldier	Mr George Dearling, W. Burton, Pulborough, Sussex	MS
Salisbury Plain	Mr Ruff, Sutton, Petworth, Sussex	JFSS 17, p. 323
Cupid the ploughboy	Mr Ruff, Sutton	MS

Title	Joint Collection	Singer and Location Source	Published?
When righteous Joseph wedded was		Mr Ruff, Sutton	MS
The American King[3]		Mrs Cranstone, Billingshurst, Sussex	*PG*, p. 5
Our Captain calls		Mrs Cranstone	*PG*, p. 34
A lawyer he rode out		Mrs Cranstone	MS
Isle of France		Mrs Cranstone	MS
A lawyer fine and gay		Mrs Cranstone	MS
Botany Bay		Mrs Cranstone	MS
The cruel father and affectionate lovers		Mrs Cranstone	MS
The true lover's farewell		Mrs Cranstone	*FSS*, p. 22
Green bushes		Mr Cranstone	*PG*, p. 16; *FMJ*, pp. 106–7
Green bushes		Mr Puttock, Sutton, Pulborough, Sussex	*FMJ*, p. 106
Jack Williams		Mr Hoare, Houghton, Sussex	MS
Cupid the ploughboy		Mr Jim Jillson, Askham Bryan, Yorkshire	*JFSS* 17, p. 336
The Irish girl		Mr Jim Jillson	MS
The bonny bunch of roses, oh!		Mr Whitehead, Heslington, Yorkshire	MS
William Taylor		Mr Whitehead	MS
The Irish girl		Mr Leatham, Askham Bryan, Yorkshire	MS

[3] Some verses are almost identical with 'The Cuckoo' in *Folk Songs from Sussex*; but the tunes are quite different.

		MS
Seventeen come Sunday	Mr Leatham	
September 1907		
It's of a farmer all in this town+ FJ	Mr William Smith, Stoke Lacy, Herefordshire	*PG*, p. 22
Little brown jug + FJ	Mr William Smith	*PG*, p. 28
Johnny Harte	Mr William Smith	MS
Shule Agra	Mr William Smith	MS
Isle of France	Mr William Smith	MS
	(also Broseley, Shropshire)	
The trees they do grow high	Mr William Smith, Stoke Lacy, Herefordshire	MS
William (Willie) the waterboy	Mr William Smith, Stoke Lacy, Herefordshire	MS
	(also Broseley, Shropshire)	
Highland soldier	Mr William Smith, Stoke Lacy, Herefordshire	MS
	(also Broseley, Shropshire)	
Bonny blue handkerchief	Mr Dick Anthony	MS
Isle of France	Mr Dick Anthony	MS
Erin's lovely home	Mr Dick Anthony	MS
Sweet primroses	Mr Dick Anthony	MS
William Taylor	Mr Jim Bull, Bishop's Frome, Herefordshire	MS
Come my own one	'Worcester Peg', Stoke Lacy, Herefordshire	MS
December 1907		
All round my hat	Mr Edmund Knight, Washington, Sussex	*PG*, p. 4
The seeds of love	Mrs Golds, Washington, Sussex	MS
Jack and the game	Mrs Golds	MS
Our Captain calls	Mrs Golds	MS

Title	Joint Collection	Singer and Location Source	Published?
?December 1907			
Black velvet band	+ FJ	Mr Standing, Washington, Sussex	MS
Just as the tide was flowing		Mr Standing	MS
Down in our village	+ FJ	Mr Standing	MS
Spanish ladies	+ FJ	Mr Cooper, Washington, Sussex	MS
Down in our village		Mrs Verrall, Horsham, Sussex	MS
Seventeen come Sunday		Mrs Verrall	MS
Dabbling in the dew		Mrs Verrall	MS
A lawyer he went out	+ FJ	Mrs Verrall	*FSS*, p. 10
Tarry trowsers	+ FJ	Mrs Verrall	*FSS*, p. 24
Come all you jolly ploughboys		Mr George Dearling, W. Burton, Pulborough, Sussex	MS
The ploughboy's glory		Mr George Dearling	MS
Barbara Allen		Mr George Dearling	MS
Sovay		Mrs Cranstone, Billinghurst, Sussex	MS
March 1908			
Cupid the ploughboy ('words not noted')		Mr Young, Bilbrough, Yorkshire	*JFSS* 17, p. 336
God rest you merry		Mr Lockly, High Ercall, Shropshire	*JFSS* 17, p. 338
Green mossy banks of the Lea		Mr Lockly	*PG*, p. 18
You seamen bold		Mr Lockly	MS
Fair maid walking down in the garden		Mr Lockly	MS

April 1908			
Jack and the game		Mr Lockly	MS
As I roamed out		Mrs Whiting, Broseley, Shropshire	*PG*, p. 6
The trees they do grow high		Mrs Whiting, Newport, Monmouthshire (now Gwent) (words from Mr William Smith)	*PG*, p. 44
Willie (William) the waterboy		Mrs Whiting, Newport, Monmouthshire (now Gwent) (also Broseley, Shropshire)	*PG*, p. 48
As I roamed out		Mr William Smith, Broseley, Shropshire	MS
Belt on, brave boys		Mr William Smith, Newport, Monmouthshire	MS
Bonny blooming Highland Jane		Mrs Whiting, Newport, Monmouthshire (also Broseley, Shropshire)	MS
July 1908			
The young and single sailor	+ FJ	Mr H. Hunt, E. Chiltington, Sussex	*JFSS* 15, p. 129
You seamen bold	+ FJ	Mr H. Hunt	*JFSS* 17, p. 322
Highland soldier		Mr H. Hunt	MS
Fair maid walking down in the garden		Mr H. Hunt	MS
The banks of green willow		Mr Cornford, E. Chiltington, Sussex	*FMJ*, p. 104
Sovay		Mr Welfare, E. Chiltington, Sussex	MS
?July 1908			
Young Caley		Mr Welfare	MS

Title	Joint Collection	Singer and Location Source	Published?
'Twas by the town of Weddingmore		Unnamed singer, Brill, Buckinghamshire	MS
September 1908			
The painful plough	+ FJ	Unnamed singer, E. Chiltington, Sussex	MS
November 1908			
Come all you little streamers	+ FJ	Mr Edwin ('Ned') Spooner, Midhurst, Sussex	*JFSS* 17, p. 310
Green bushes	+ FJ	Mr Edwin ('Ned') Spooner	*FMJ*, p. 107
'Twas of a brisk and lively lad	+ FJ	Mr Edwin ('Ned') Spooner	MS
December 1908			
The bold fisherman	+ FJ	Mr Edwin ('Ned') Spooner	*PG*, p. 10
The ploughboy's glory	+ FJ	Mr Edwin ('Ned') Spooner	MS
The basket of eggs	+ FJ	Mr Edwin ('Ned') Spooner	MS
?1908			
A brisk young sailor courted me	+ FJ	Mr Ford, Scaynes Hill, Sussex'	*FSS*, p. 16
January 1909 Henry Martin ('words collected in Horsham')		Mr G. Hillman, Shoreham, Sussex	*JFSS* 17, p. 301
Sweet primroses		Unnamed singer, Shoreham, Sussex	MS

Date / Song	Singer		Source
February 1909 Botany Bay	Mr Turner, Sheffield Park, Sussex	+ FJ	MS
March 1909 The pretty ploughboy ('words were not noted')	Mr G. Hillman, Shoreham, Sussex		*JFSS* 17, p. 303
June 1909 Down by the greenwood side	Mr Verrall, Horsham, Sussex		*JFSS* 17, p. 281
Spanish ladies	Mr Verrall		MS
Fourteen years of age	Mr Verrall		MS
A blacksmith courted me	Mr Verrall		*JFSS* 17; *FSS* p.16
?June 1909 Lord Bateman	Mr Verrall		MS
Geordie	Mr Verrall		MS
July 1909 Lord Carter is my name	Mrs Cranstone, Billingshurst, Sussex		*JFSS* 17, p. 290
A brisk young sailor[4]	Mrs Cranstone		*FMJ*, p. 105
Twankydillo	Mrs Cranstone		MS
?July 1909 Young Caley	Mrs Cranstone		MS

[4] *Cf.* the tune as noted by Jekyll in *Folk Songs from Sussex.*

Title	Joint Collection	Singer and Location Source	Published?
'Twas by the town of Weddingmore		Mr Cranstone	*JFSS* 17, p. 341
In the famous town of Nottingham		Mr Cranstone	MS
The rambling sailor		Mr Verrall, Horsham, Sussex	*PG*, p. 36
Thomas Hegan and Sally Blair		Mr Verrall	*PG*, p. 43
Phoebe and her dark-eyed sailor		Mr Verrall	MS
All round my hat		Mr Verrall	MS
Whilst old Engeland's a going down the hill		Mr Verrall	MS
The lads of Kilkenny		Mr Bill Wix, Billingshurst, Sussex	MS
It's an old miser in London did dwell		Mr Bill Wix	MS
The cuckoo		Mr Bill Wix	*FSS*, p. 14
?1909			
Yonder stands a lovely creature	+ FJ	Mr Martin, Fletching, Sussex	*FSS*, p. 14
We poor labouring men	+ FJ	Unnamed singer, East Meon, Hampshire	*PG*, p. 46

April 1910			
Fair Phoebe and her dark-eyed sailor	+ FJ	Mr George ('Chummy') Goble, Filby, Norfolk	*JFSS* 15, p. 131
Fair Phoebe and her dark-eyed sailor	+ FJ	Mr George Locke, Rollesby, Norfolk	*JFSS* 15, p. 132
The bold fisherman		Mr George Locke	MS
The bonny bunch of roses, oh!	+ FJ	Mr James Landamore, Wroxham, Norfolk	MS
The molecatcher	+ FJ	Mr James Landamore	*JFSS* 15, p. 87
The tinker	+ FJ	Mr James Landamore	MS
Green mossy banks of the Lea	+ FJ	Mr James Landamore	MS
Admiral Benbow	+ FJ	Mr 'Skinny' (or 'Skinner') Crow, Filby, Norfolk	MS
Isle of France	+ FJ	Mr 'Skinny' ('Skinner') Crow	MS
A sailor in the north countree	+ FJ	Mr 'Skinny' ('Skinner') Crow	MS
August 1910			
An old man he courted me	+ FJ	Mrs Powell, Minster, Sheppey, Kent	*PG*, p. 32
September 1910			
The bold fisherman		Unnamed singer, Minster, Sheppey, Kent	MS
Bold General Wolfe		Unnamed singer, Minster, Sheppey, Kent	MS
Bold Princess Royal		Unnamed singer, Minster, Sheppey, Kent	MS
23 and 25 October 1910			
Lovely Joan (phonograph used)	+ VW	Mr William Hurr, Southwold, Suffolk	*JFSS* 17, p. 330

Title	Joint Collection	Singer and Location Source	Published?
24 October 1910			
The Wreck of the Royal George	+VW	Mr Robert Hurr, Southwold, Suffolk	MS
25 October 1910			
When I was bound apprentice	+VW	Mr William Hurr, Southwold, Suffolk	*JFSS* 17, p. 329
The loss of the London	+VW	Mr William Hurr	*JFSS* 17, p. 331.
Geordie	+VW	Mr Newby, Reydon, Suffolk	*JFSS* 17, p. 332
New garden fields ('corrected from a phonograph record [. . .]. The intonation of this song was peculiar and difficult to note')	+VW	Mr George Locke, Rollesby, Norfolk	*JFSS* 17, p. 334
Green mossy banks of the Lea	+VW	Mr George Locke	MS
Just as the tide was flowing	+VW	Mr George Locke	MS
Liverpool play	+VW	Mr George Locke	MS
?25 October 1910			
Birmingham town	+VW	Mr George Locke	MS
The basket of eggs	+VW	Mr George Locke	MS
25 and 26 October 1910			
The captain's apprentice	+VW	Mr George ('Chummy') Goble, Filby, Norfolk	*JFSS* 17, p. 335

Song		Singer / Place	Source
Roger the miller	+ VW	Mr George ('Chummy') Goble	MS
October 1910			
The murder of Maria Marten		Mr Keble, Shadingfield, Suffolk	MS
Forty miles		Mr Newby, Reydon, Suffolk	MS
Bold Princess Royal	+ VW	Mr Robert Hurr, Southwold, Suffolk	MS
Liverpool Hornpipe (played on concertina)	+ VW	Mr Robert Hurr	MS
When Jones' ale was new	+ VW	Mr Ben Hurr, Southwold, Suffolk	MS
On Monday morning I married a wife	+ VW	Mr ? Hurr, Southwold, Suffolk	MS
Young Collins	+ FJ	Mr Greenfield, Lurgashall, Sussex	*PG*, p. 49
Jack goes up to London	+ FJ	Mr Greenfield	*FMJ*, p. 112
November 1910			
Yonder stands a lovely creature		Mr Heygate, Rusper, Sussex	MS
The basket of eggs		Mr Heygate, Rusper, Sussex	MS
Jack went up to London city	+ FJ	Mr Heygate	*PG*, p. 24
August 1911			
God rest you merry		Mrs Cranstone, Billingshurst, Sussex	*JFSS* 17, p. 339
?1911			
Week before Easter		Mrs Cranstone	MS
The wreck of the Royal George		Mr Verrall, Horsham, Sussex	MS

Title	Joint Collection	Singer and Location Source	Published?
19 December 1911			
The keys of Heaven	+ VW	Mr Woods, Tibenham, Norfolk	PG, p. 26
20 December 1911			
As Robin was driving	+ VW	Mr 'Blue' Fisher, Tibenham, Norfolk	PG, p. 8
Horse racing song	+ VW	Mr 'Blue' Fisher	PG, p. 20; FMJ, pp. 109
December 1911			
Harvest song	+ VW	Mr Jack Dade, Pulham, Norfolk	JFSS 17, p. 347
The servant man		Mr Walter Searle	PG, p. 42
'Twas down in yonder valley		Mr Walter Searle, Wepham, Sussex	MS
June 1912			
Merry Bloomfield		Unnamed singer, Ipswich, Suffolk	PG, p. 29
William Taylor		Unnamed singer, Ipswich, Suffolk	PG, p. 45
Tree in the wood		Unnamed singer, Ipswich, Suffolk	MS
March 1913 or April 1910			
Crystal stream	+ FJ?	Mr 'Skinny' (or 'Skinner') Crow, Filby, Norfolk	PG, p. 13
Gipsy Laddy O	+ FJ?	Mr 'Skinny' (or 'Skinner') Crow	PG, p. 14
March 1913			
On the first of November		Mr 'Skinny' (or 'Skinner') Crow	PG, p. 30
Saucy Ward		Mr 'Skinny' (or 'Skinner') Crow	PG, p. 38

Spanish ladies	Young sailor, Winterton, Norfolk	MS
A story, a story	Mr John Woodhouse, California, Ormesby, Norfolk	*PG*, p. 40
On the first of November	Mr John Woodhouse	MS
?March 1913		
O father, dear father	Mr John Woodhouse	MS
?		
Scarbro' Town	Unnamed singer and location	MS
Sowing the seeds of love	Mrs Cranstone, Billingshurst, Sussex	*FSS*, p. 8

Appendix Three

BUTTERWORTH'S WRITINGS

Articles on Bowen, Dunhill and Balfour Gardiner in *Grove's Dictionary of Music and Musicians*, 2nd (1904–10), 3rd (1927), 4th (1940) and 5th (1954) editions, Macmillan, London; articles on Bowen and Dunhill retained in *The New Grove Dictionary of Music and Musicians*, Vols 3 and 5, Macmillan, London, 1980.

Diary of Morris-Dance Hunting, April 1912, Vol. 10 in the Butterworth Manuscripts, Cecil Sharp House, London.

The Country Dance Book (Parts 3 and 4, with Cecil Sharp), Novello, London, 1912 and 1916; after various editions and revisions, reprinted by E. P. Publishing Ltd, Wakefield, 1975, and subsequently by A. & C. Black, London, 1984, and Harry Styles, Carshalton, 1985; published in connection with *Country Dance Tunes*, Sets 5 to 8, and containing 35 (Part 3) and 45 (Part 4) country dances from *The English Dancing Master*, described by Sharp and Butterworth.[1]

The Morris Book (Part 5, with Cecil Sharp), Novello, 1913; reprinted by E. P. Publishing Ltd, Wakefield, 1975, and subsequently by A. & C. Black, London, 1984, and Harry Styles, Carshalton, 1985; published in connection with *Morris Dance Tunes*, Books 9 and 10.[2]

'Vaughan Williams' *London Symphony*', *RCM Magazine*, Vol. 10, No. 2, Easter Term 1914, pp. 44–6; reprinted in *Memorial Volume*, pp. 95–96.[3]

---

[1] *Cf.* p. 87.

[2] *Cf.* pp. 87 and 88.

[3] *Cf.* pp. 169–171.

Programme notes for the London premieres of *A Shropshire Lad* Rhapsody and *The Banks of Green Willow*, 20 March 1914; reprinted in *Memorial Volume*, pp. 114–15.

Programme notes for the premiere of Vaughan Williams' *A London Symphony*, 27 March 1914.

'The Songs and Dances in *A Midsummer Night's Dream* at the Savoy Theatre', *Journal of the English Folk-Dance Society*, Vol. 1, No. 1, May 1914, pp. 12–13.[4]

War Diary and extracts from letters, August 1914–July 1916, *Memorial Volume*, pp. 15–80.

[4] *Cf.* pp. 166–68.

Appendix Four

THE SONGS AND DANCES
IN *A MIDSUMMER NIGHT'S DREAM*
AT THE SAVOY THEATRE

Cecil Sharp's original men's morris side gave the first stage performance of folk dancing in December 1912 at the Savoy Theatre,
encouraged by Harley Granville Barker, who had the use of the
theatre for his Shakespeare productions. The following season saw
the amalgamation of Shakespeare and folk dancing, as witnessed in
this account by George Butterworth in the *Journal of the English Folk-
Dance Society*, Vol. 1, No. 1, May 1914.

It is not hard to account for the exceptional interest taken in this
production. Of all Shakespeare's plays, *A Midsummer Night's Dream*
requires, perhaps, the most delicate stage-handling, and, after the
undoubted success of *Twelfth Night*, everyone was anxious to see
how Mr. Barker would fare with his latest choice. Moreover, the co-
operation of Mr. Cecil Sharp was an event of some importance,
seeing that the effect of this particular play depends in no small
measure upon the music and dances employed.

It is with these that this article is concerned; and yet, since they
are not merely imported, but arranged specially for this production, they cannot be dealt with altogether apart from their
context.

So much has already been written about the 'All-Gold' fairies,
that it is unnecessary to dwell upon the extremely exotic character
of their appearance. Apart from costume, the most remarkable
thing about them is the grotesque jerkiness with which they move –
an idea presumably borrowed from certain of the later Russian
ballets. Their first entry sets one wondering what possible use Mr.
Barker can have for Mr. Sharp, who is above all things the apostle of
'natural movements'. It very soon transpires that the compromise
arrived at is that the 'marionette' style shall prevail so long as there
is no music to control the action, but that when the dancing begins,

it shall be in the manner, more or less, of ordinary human beings.

It is hardly necessary to point out the inconsistency of this arrangement; Mr. Barker's idea might be successful if he had Nijinsky to help in carrying it out; Mr. Sharp's dances are beautiful in themselves, and might pass as fairy dances if the stage-illusion were more credible.

Of these dances the most elaborate, and perhaps the most effective, is that performed round and about Titania's mound; this dance begins and ends with a simple 'hands-all' round the central figure, and in between come a number of figures of the well-known Playford type, but considerably elaborated, and combined with the greatest ingenuity; particularly noteworthy is the way in which the twelve dancers are made to divide into groups first of six, then of three, then of six again, and finally back into the original ring.

In this and the other dances the steps used are of the simplest possible kind, but the body movements have evidently been carefully thought out, and serve to emphasise the ceremonial nature of the performance.

Mention must also be made of the 'Bergomask' danced by Bottom and two others of his company; for this Mr. Sharp has simply borrowed the Wyresdale *Greensleeves*, which seems as if made for the purpose, and is quite the popular thing of the evening.

As to the music, there can surely be no room for doubt; the appropriateness of the folk-tunes used is unquestionable, and their simple arrangement for an orchestra consisting of flute, horn, harpsichord and string-quartet gives just the right amount of background both for song and dance. The actual dance-tunes used are – *Sellenger's Round*, *Greensleeves*, *The Triumph*, *Chestnut* and *Nonesuch*.

The song 'Ye spotted snakes' is set to a fine carol-melody, and its chorus ('Philomel with melody') to another equally beautiful folk-tune.

The 'Still Music' in Act IV consists of an instrumental arrangement of *The Sprig of Thyme* (Somerset version), but is rather spoiled by the loudness of the speaking voices.

In only one case has Mr. Sharp had recourse to original composition; the closing scene of the play requires a 'song and dance' combined, no words being given in the text; the choice of the unfamiliar lyric 'Roses, their sharp spines' is a good one, and of Mr. Sharp's setting it is high praise to be able to say that it forms a fitting prelude to the series of beautiful tunes into which it leads.

On the whole, those interested in the revival of our folk-dances may have good reason to feel satisfied with this the first serious attempt to adapt them for stage purposes. It is true that their elaboration is not carried very far, the play not requiring it; but the possibility of a more specifically dramatic development is clearly foreshadowed. The 'mound' dance, for instance, shows the fairies doing homage to Titania – an idea quite beyond the province of the folk-dance proper, but one which Mr. Sharp finds no difficulty in expressing by means of familiar movements. Again, in the closing scene, the way in which the fairies gradually dance themselves off is not a mere technical device for clearing the stage; the whole spirit of Oberon's farewell speech seems to be embodied in it, and the disappearance of the last fairy, synchronising with the return of the 'Philomel' tune, is perhaps the most memorable moment in the whole performance.

It cannot be doubted that if ever the opportunity occurs for a truly national production of ballet or opera, the success of the undertaking will rest in the hands of those who have mastered the technique and absorbed the spirit of our English dances and songs.

Appendix Five

VAUGHAN WILLIAMS'
LONDON SYMPHONY

George Butterworth wrote this article for *RCM Magazine*, the magazine of the Royal College of Music after the premiere of the Symphony on 27 March 1914. It was a work Butterworth knew intimately from the beginning, and nobody was better suited to writing a critical appreciation of it.

Mr F. B. Ellis, whose recent series of concerts is noticed elsewhere, may be considered fortunate in having secured the first performance of at least one work of outstanding importance. The compositions of Vaughan Williams merit the attention of every serious student, not merely on account of their intrinsic musical value, but also as affording an unusually interesting example of the growth of a contemporary style. It would be hard to name any other first-rate composer who has 'found himself' with such apparent difficulty as Vaughan Williams, and this fact is sometimes cited against him as a proof of amateurish clumsiness; the beauty and originality of his ideas is widely recognised, but the not infrequent failure to express them clearly is usually ascribed to some inherent incapacity for perfecting a technique.

It would probably be more logical to blame the actual newness of the ideas themselves, and the necessity thus created for the laborious working out of a new method. The same paradox applies in some measure to all composers of progressive tendency, but in the case of Vaughan Williams the labours of the preceding generation seem to have been unusually little assistance; the absence of a characteristically native idiom may largely account for this, but it would be premature to attempt a final explanation. What is of more immediate importance is to recognize that in his later works Vaughan Williams has given evidence of having finally overcome what Mr Edwin Evans aptly terms his 'impediment of musical speech'; hence the announcement of a full-blooded symphony

from his pen was calculated to raise hopes of something exception-
ally good.

It may be said at once that these hopes have been fully realized; in
this new work, almost for the first time, the composer's ideas and
their actual expression are really commensurate, and the success of
the symphony was greatly enhanced by the magnificent performance given by the Queen's Hall Orchestra, under the direction of
Mr Geoffrey Toye – perhaps as good a 'first performance' as it
would be possible to obtain.

As its title implies, the symphony is descriptive of London, more
especially the London of to-day. It would be useless, without the aid
of musical illustrations, to give an exhaustive analysis, and a short
account of each movement must sufffice.

A slow, mystical prelude – to be considered as introductory to the
work as a whole – leads directly into the first movement proper, an
exhilarating and expansive piece of music, which seems to owe its
genesis to the stirring bustle of every-day life, and the busy turmoil
of the London streets. The melodic material is very abundant, and
many of the tunes have a distinctly 'popular' flavour about them;
there are, of course, contrasting sections of more restrained character, but the general mood is boisterous, and the close a perfect
orgy of triumph. This movement is certainly the most brilliant piece
of orchestral writing that Vaughan Williams has as yet produced.

The slow movement is an idyll of grey skies and secluded by-
ways – an aspect of London quite as familiar as any other; the
feeling of the music is remote and mystical, and its very characteristic beauty is not of a kind which it is possible to describe in
words.

To the Scherzo is given the alternative title 'Nocturne'; the
combination is unexpected, but justified by the nature of the
subject; after all, to the average Londoner, the night is generally the
time in which he is free to 'play'. It is not, however, a scene of
conventional metropolitan gaiety which is depicted, but rather the
careless freedom with which common folk disport themselves at
night in the open streets. In addition to the 'Scherzo' proper there
are two 'Trios', of which the second is in strong contrast with the
rest of the movement.

The Finale is the longest of the four movements; perhaps, also, it
is the least satisfactory; not that there is any falling off in the
interest, but, as in the last movement of the 'Sea' Symphony, there
is a feeling that the composer is straining himself to express just a
little too much; in this case, however, the flaw is a much slighter
one, and may easily prove to be illusory when the work is heard a

second time. The music is for the most part strenuous, but in a different sense from that in which the first movement is so. It is the unrest of a conscious struggle which is here suggested.

When this mood has worked itself out, there is a return to the theme of the Prelude, which is treated at some length, and forms an impressive epilogue to the whole work.

It is now also a common-place to say of a novelty that it was 'enthusiastically received'; the description means little or nothing, and yet there are occasions on which it is instinctively and generally felt that something out of the ordinary has been achieved. There can be no question as to the appeal which this work made to those who were present on March 27, and it is presumable that it would be equally successful with any normal English audience. The only question is whether it will be given the opportunity of becoming popular. The mere necessity for asking such a question shows up once again the astonishing conditions which govern the policy of concert-giving organizations in this country, and it is actually true that no arrangements have as yet been made for a second performance.

Appendix Six

DISCOGRAPHY

1. *Two English Idylls*

(a) English Sinfonia/Neville Dilkes, HMV CSD 3705 (LP), April 1972 (recorded June 1971) (with Warlock, *Capriol Suite*; Ireland, *The Holy Boy*; Leigh, *Harpsichord Concertino*; Moeran, *Lonely Waters, Whythorne's Shadow*); re-issued 1981 on HMV (TC) 7101 (LP).

(b) London Philharmonic Orchestra/Sir Adrian Boult. Lyrita SRCS 69 (LP), January 1976 (with Rhapsody, *A Shropshire Lad, The Banks of Green Willow* and, with the New Philharmonia Orchestra, Howells, *Merry Eye, Music for a Prince, Elegy* for viola, string quartet and string orchestra)

(c) Academy of St Martin-in-the-Fields/Neville Marriner. Argo ZRG 860 (LP; cassette KZRC 860), November 1976 (with Rhapsody, *A Shropshire Lad, The Banks of Green Willow*; Britten, *Variations on a Theme of Frank Bridge*); also issued on D 26 D 4 (LP).

(d) English Chamber Orchestra/Jeffrey Tate, HMV Digital EL 27 05921 (LP), 1987 (recorded August 1985); CDC 7 47945-2 (CD); EL 270592-4 (cassette). (with *The Banks of Green Willow*, Bridge, *There is a willow grows aslant a brook*; Moeran, *Lonely Waters, Whythorne's Shadow*; Bax, *Evening Piece, Irish Landscape, Dance in the Sunlight*).

(e) English String Orchestra/William Boughton, Nimbus Digital NI 5068 (CD) and NC 5068 (cassette), 1986 (with *The Banks of Green Willow*, the Rhapsody, *A Shropshire Lad*, Bridge, *Suite for Strings*; Parry, *Lady Radnor's Suite*).

(f) Royal Liverpool Philharmonic Orchestra/Grant Llewellyn, Argo 436 401-2ZH (CD), May 1993 (with *The Banks of Green Willow*, Rhapsody, *A Shropshire Lad*; Coleridge Taylor, *Ballade* in

A minor, *Symphonic Variations on an African Air*; MacCunn, *Land of the Mountain and the Flood*).

2. Rhapsody, *A Shropshire Lad*

(a) British Symphony Orchestra/Adrian Boult, HMV D 520 (78 rpm), Spring 1921.

(b) Hallé Orchestra/Sir Adrian Boult, HMV C 3287 (78 rpm), June 1942; re-issued on HMV Treasury, ED 291 092-1.

(c) ABC Sydney Symphony Orchestra/Eugene Goossens, HMV DB 9792/3 (78 rpm), 1952. (with Grainger (arr.), *The Londonderry Air*).

(d) London Philharmonic Orchestra/Sir Adrian Boult, Decca LXT 5015 (LP), April 1955 (recorded 1 November 1954) (with *The Banks of Green Willow*; Bax, *Tintagel*; Holst, *The Perfect Fool* Ballet Music; re-issued (i) on LW 5175 (10" LP) (with Holst, *The Perfect Fool* Ballet Music); re-issued (ii) May 1964 (deleted 1972) on ACL 224 (LP) (with *The Banks of Green Willow*; Walton, Overture: *Portsmouth Point, Siesta*; Elgar, *Wand of Youth* Suite No. 1); re-issued (iii) September 1972 on ECS 647 (LP) (with *The Banks of Green Willow*; Bax, *Tintagel*; Vaughan Williams, Overture: *The Wasps*; Walton, Overture: *Portsmouth Point, Siesta*, Overture: *Scapino*).

(e) Hallé Orchestra/Sir John Barbirolli, Pye CCT 31000 (10" LP), July 1957 (with Bax, *The Garden of Fand*); re-issued (i) May 1966 on Pye GSGC 14061 (LP) (with Bax, *The Garden of Fand*; Vaughan Williams, Symphony No. 8); re-issued (ii) 1975 on Pye GSGC 15017 (LP) (Collector Series) (with Bax, *The Garden of Fand*; Vaughan Williams, Symphony No. 8; re-issued (iii) on PVCD 8380 (LP)).

(f) English Sinfonia/Neville Dilkes, HMV CSD 3696 (LP), December 1971 (recorded June 1971) (with *The Banks of Green Willow*; Bridge, *There is a willow grows aslant a brook*; Harty, *John Field Suite*; Bax, *Dance in the Sunlight*); re-issued (i) February 1981 on ESD 7100 (LP; cassette TC ESD 7100); re-issued (ii) on cassette EMI TC 2-MOM 104 (*Greensleeves*) (with Vaughan Williams, *Fantasia on Greensleeves, The Lark Ascending*, Oboe Concerto, *English Folk-Song Suite*; Delius, *Walk to the Paradise Garden, On Hearing the First Cuckoo in Spring*; Elgar, *Serenade for Strings*; Moeran, *Lonely Waters*; various conductors and orchestras).

(g) London Philharmonic Orchestra/Sir Adrian Boult. Lyrita SRCS 69 (LP), January 1976 (for details of couplings *cf.* 1 (b)).

(h) Academy of St Martin-in-the-Fields/Neville Marriner, Argo ZRG 860 (LP; cassette KZRC 860), November 1976 (for details of couplings *cf.* 1 (c)); also issued on D 26 D 4 (LP).

(i) English String Orchestra/William Boughton, Nimbus Digital NI 5068 (CD) (for details of couplings *cf.* 1 (e)).

(j) English Symphony Orchestra, English String Orchestra/ William Boughton (*The Spirit of England*). Nimbus NI 5210-13 (four CDs), NC 5210-13 (four cassettes), 1989 (with *The Banks of Green Willow*; Finzi, *Love's Labour Lost*, Clarinet Concerto; Elgar, *Introduction and Allegro, Sospiri, Cockaigne* Overture; Vaughan Williams, *Fantasia on a Theme of Thomas Tallis, Fantasia on Greensleeves*, Oboe Concerto, *The Lark Ascending*; Holst, *St Paul's Suite*; Britten, *Variations on a Theme of Frank Bridge*; Bridge, *Suite for Strings*; Parry, *Lady Radnor's Suite*; Warlock, *Capriol Suite*; Delius, *Summer Evening*).

(k) Royal Liverpool Philharmonic Orchestra/Grant Llewellyn, (for details of couplings, *cf.* 1(f)).

3. *The Banks of Green Willow*

(a) Philharmonia Orchestra/Maurice Miles, HMV C 3491 (LP), date unknown.

(b) London Philharmonic Orchestra/Sir Adrian Boult, Decca LXT 5015 (LP), April 1955 (recorded 1 November 1954); re-issued (i) May 1964 on ACL 224 (LP); re-issued (ii) September 1972 on ECS 647 (LP) (for details of couplings on all three recordings *cf.* 2 (d)).

(c) English Sinfonia/Neville Dilkes, HMV CSD 3696 (LP), December 1971 (recorded June 1971) (for details of couplings and reissues *cf.* 2 (f)).

(d) London Philharmonic Orchestra/Sir Adrian Boult, Lyrita SRCS 69 (LP), January 1976 (for details of couplings *cf.* 1 (b)).

(e) Academy of St Martin-in-the-Fields/Neville Marriner, Argo ZRG 860 (LP; cassette KZRC 860) November 1976 (For details of couplings *cf.* 1 (c)); also issued on D 26 D 4 (LP). re-issued July 1982 on Argo ZRG 945 (LP; cassette KZRC 945), (with Delius, *On Hearing the First Cuckoo in Spring*; Elgar, *Serenade for Strings*; Vaughan Williams, *Fantasia on a Theme of Thomas Tallis*; Warlock, *Capriol Suite*).

(f) London Symphony Orchestra/André Previn (*André Previn's Music Night 2*), HMV ASD 3338 (LP; cassette TCC 2-POR 54290), 1977 (with Glinka, Overture: *Russlan and Ludmilla*; Barber, *Adagio for Strings*; Falla, Suite No. 2 from *The Three-Cornered Hat*; Debussy, *Prélude à l'après-midi d'un faune*; J. Strauss II, *Emperor Waltz*.

(g) Bournemouth Sinfonietta/Norman del Mar, RCA RL 25184 (LP), 1979 (with Bantock, *The Pierrot of the Minute*; Bridge, *Summer, There is a willow grows aslant a brook* and *Suite for Strings*); also issued on (i) Chandos CBR 1018 (LP) and CHAN 8373 (CD), CBT 1018 (cassette), (ii) on Conifer ASPC (cassette/ASPD 3067 (CD), 1991, under the title *England's Green and Pleasant Lands*.

(h) English Chamber Orchestra/Jeffrey Tate, HMV Digital EL 27 05921 (LP), CDC 7 47945-2 (CD), EL 270592-4 (cassette), 1987 (for details of couplings *cf.* 1 (d)).

(i) English String Orchestra/William Boughton, Nimbus Digital NI 5068 (CD), NC 5068 (cassette) (for details of couplings *cf.* 1 (e)).

4. *I will make you brooches*

Graham Trew (baritone), Roger Vignoles (piano), Hyperion A66037 (LP), May 1982 (recorded June 1981) (with *Requiescat, I fear thy kisses, A lawyer he went out, Roving in the dew, The true lover's farewell, Bredon Hill and Other Songs* and Vaughan Williams, *Songs of Travel*).

5. *I fear thy kisses*

Graham Trew, Roger Vignoles, Hyperion A66037 (LP), May 1982 (recorded June 1981) (for details of couplings *cf.* 4).

6. *Six Songs from 'A Shropshire Lad'*

(a) Keith Falkner (bass-baritone), Gerald Moore (piano), HMV B 9064 (78 rpm), recorded June 1940 (one song only: 'Is my team ploughing?') (with Somervell, *The street sounds to the soldier's tread*); re-issued 1971 on HMV HQM 1238 (LP) ('Golden Voice' Series, No. 21) (with songs and arias by Purcell, Handel, Mendelssohn, Elgar, Somervell, Peel and others).

(b) Roy Henderson (baritone), Gerald Moore (piano), Decca M

506/7 (78 rpm), 1941; re-issued September 1979 on Decca ECM 834 (LP) (with songs from Walton, *Façade* (Edith Sitwell, Constant Lambert, chamber ensemble/Walton) and Finzi, *Dies Natalis* (Joan Cross, Boyd Neel Orchestra/Boyd Neel)).

(c) John Cameron (baritone), Gerald Moore (piano), HMV DLP 1117 (10" LP), 1956 (with *Bredon Hill and Other Songs*).

(d) Peter Pears (tenor), Benjamin Britten (piano), Decca LW 5241 (10" LP) ((LP) Volume 3 of *An Anthology of English Song*), June 1956 (one song only: 'Is my team ploughing?') (with Berkeley, *How love came in*; Bridge, *Go not, happy day*, *Love went a-riding*; Holst, *Persephone*; Ireland, *I have twelve oxen*; Moeran, *In youth is pleasure*; Warlock, *Yarmouth Fair*; Britten, *Let the florid music praise*; Oldham, *3 Chinese Lyrics*). Re-issued (i) September 1960 on BR 3066 (10" LP) (with songs by Schubert; Bridge, *Go not, happy day*; Britten, *Let the florid music praise, Before life and after*; and Dowland, Morley and Rosseter, songs; with Julian Bream (lute)); re-issued (ii) June 1970 on ECS 545 (LP) (with songs on LW 5241, and Dowland, Ford, Morley and Rosseter, songs) with Julian Bream).

(e) Wilfred Brown (tenor), Margaret McNamee (piano), Jupiter JUR 00A5 (LP), 00A5 (cassette); 1962. (one song only: 'Loveliest of trees'.) (with Warlock, W. Denis Browne, Gurney, Finzi, Berkeley, Wallace Southam and Walton, songs).

(f) John Shirley-Quirk (baritone), Martin Isepp (piano), Saga 5260 (LP), October 1966 (with Vaughan Williams, *Songs of Travel, Linden Lea, Silent Noon*; Keel, *Trade Winds*; Stanford, *Drake's Drum*; Warlock, *Captain Stratton's Fancy*; Ireland, *Sea Fever*; with Viola Tunnard (piano); Ireland, *My Fair, I have twelve oxen, The Sally Gardens, Love and Friendship* with Eric Parkin (piano)); re-issued (i) one song only: 'Loveliest of trees') on Saga 5349 (LP); re-issued (ii) November 1980 on Saga 5473 (LP).

(g) Frederick Harvey (baritone), Gerald Moore (piano), HMV 3587 (LP), 1967 (one song only: 'Loveliest of trees') (with Somervell, *The street sounds*; Elgar, *Shepherd's Song*; Holst, 'Varuna I' ('Sky') from *Vedic Hymns*, Group I; Bridge, *O that it were so*; Vaughan Williams, *Silent Noon*; Quilter, *O mistress mine*; Bax, *The white peace*; Gurney, *I will go with my father a-ploughing*; Head, *Ludlow Town*; Warlock, *Autumn Twilight*; Finzi, *Come away, Death*; Gibbs, *Silver*; Bliss, *Rich or Poor*; Britten, *The Birds*; Ireland, *When lights go rolling round the sky*) re-issued on HMV Greensleeve ESD 7054 (LP).

(h) Anthony Rolfe Johnson (tenor), David Willison (piano), Polydor Select 2460 245 (LP), January 1976 (with songs by Ireland, Warlock and Gurney).

(i) Benjamin Luxon (baritone), David Willison (piano), Argo ZRG 838 (LP), April 1976 (with *Bredon Hill and Other Songs*, and Finzi, *Earth and Air and Rain*).

(j) John Carol Case (baritone), Daphne Ibbott (piano), Pearl SHE 527 (LP), May 1976 (with Somervell, *Maud*).

(k) Graham Trew (baritone), Roger Vignoles (piano), Meridian E77031/2 (LP) (KE 77031/2) cassette, April 1980 (recorded August 1979) (with other settings of Housman by Somervell, Moeran, Peel, C. W. Orr, Gibbs, Bax, Ireland and Gurney).

(l) David Wilson-Johnson (baritone), David Owen Norris (piano), Hyperion A66187 (LP) (with Somervell, *Maud*).

(m) Thomas Allen (baritone), Geoffrey Parsons (piano), Virgin VC 7 91105-2 (CD), *On the Idle Hill of Summer* (title of disc), 1990 (with Vaughan Williams, *The House of Life*; Peel, *In Summertime on Bredon*; Quilter, *Seven Elizabethan Lyrics*; Butterworth, *On the Idle Hill of Summer*; Quilter, *Now Sleeps the Crimson Petal*; Vaughan Williams, *Linden Lea*).

(n) Benjamin Luxon (baritone), David Willison (piano). Chandos CHAN 8831 (CD) (with *Bredon Hill and Other Songs*; Gurney's *Apple Orchard, The Salley Gardens, Sleep, Hawk and Buckle, Fiddler of Dooney, On the Downs, Epitaph*).

(o) Brian Rayner Cook (baritone), Clifford Benson (piano). Unicorn-Kanchana DKP (CD) 9113, September 1991 (with Vaughan Williams, *The House of Life, In the Spring, Linden Lea, Songs of Travel*).

(p) Peter Medhurst (bass), Nicholas Durcan (piano) (*Phantasmagoria: Songs of the Supernatural in English and German*), Aeterna AET CD 911 277 (cassette AET CAS 311 127) (one song only: 'Is My Team Ploughing').

(q) Anthony Rolfe Johnson (tenor), David Willison (piano), IMP PCD 1065 (CD) (with Vaughan Williams, *Songs of Travel*; Ireland, *The Land of Lost Content*; songs by Gurney and Warlock).

(r) Bryn Terfel (baritone), Malcolm Martineau (piano), Deutsche Grammophon 445 946-2 (CD) (recorded February 1995) (with *Bredon Hill and Other Songs*; Vaughan Williams, *Songs of Travel*; Finzi, *Let Us Garlands Bring*; Ireland, *Sea Fever, The Vagabond, The Bells of San Marie*).

(s) Anthony Rolfe Johnson (tenor), Graham Johnson (piano), Alan Bates (reader), Hyperion CDA 66471/2 (two CDS) 1995 (with 'Bredon Hill', 'When the lad for longing sighs', 'On the idle hill of summer'; C. W. Orr, 'Oh see how thick the goldcup flowers', 'When I watch the living meet', 'This time of year', 'Into my heart an air that kills', *The Isle of Portland, Hughley Steeple*; Ireland, *The Heart's Desire*, 'Goal and wicket', 'The encounter', 'The Lent lily', 'The vain desire', *Hawthorne Time*, 'Epilogue'; Moeran, *Oh fair enough are sky and plain, Far in a western brookland*; Horder, *White in the moon the long road lies*; Berkeley, *Because I liked you better, He would not stay for me*; Barber, *With rue my heart is laden*).

(t) Orch. Lance Baker: Stephen Varcoe (baritone), City of London Sinfonia/Richard Hickox, Chandos CHAN 8743 (with *Love Blows as the Wind Blows*; Quilter, *Shakespeare Songs*; Elgar, *Twilight, Pleading*; Finzi, *Let Us Garlands Bring*; Vaughan Williams, *The House of Life*; Ireland, *If There Were Dreams to Sell, Hope the Hornblower*).

7. *Bredon Hill and Other Songs*

(a) John Cameron (baritone), Gerald Moore (piano), HMV DLP 1117 (10" LP), 1956 (for details of couplings, *cf.* 6 (c)).

(b) Benjamin Luxon (baritone), David Willison (piano), Argo ZRG 838, April 1976 (for details of couplings, *cf.* 6 (n)).

(c) Graham Trew (baritone), Roger Vignoles (piano). Hyperion A66037, May 1982 (recorded June 1981) (for details of couplings, *cf.* 4).

(d) Benjamin Luxon (baritone), David Willison (piano), Chandos CHAN 8831 (for details of couplings, *cf.* 6 (i)).

(e) Thomas Allen (baritone), Geoffrey Parsons (piano), Virgin VC7 91105-2 (CD), 1990 (one song only: 'On the Idle Hill of Summer') (for details of couplings, *cf.* 6(m)).

(f) Bryn Terfel (baritone), Malcolm Martineau (piano), Deutsche

Grammophon 445 946-2 (CD) (recorded February 1995) (for details of couplings, *cf.* 6(r)).

(g) Anthony Rolfe Johnson (tenor), Graham Johnson (piano), Hyperion CDA 6647 1/2 (two CDs) 1995 (three songs only: 'Bredon Hill', 'When the lad for longing sighs', 'On the idle hill of summer') (for details of couplings, *cf.* 6(s)).

8. *Requiescat*

(a) Graham Trew (baritone), Roger Vignoles (piano), Hyperion A66037 (LP), May 1982 (recorded June 1981) (for details of couplings, *cf.* 4.)

(b) Stephen Varcoe (baritone), Clifford Benson (piano), Hyperion CDA 66261/2 (CD), 1988 (recorded April 1987) (this double CD is entitled *War Embers*, and also features songs by Gurney (28), Finzi (1), W. Denis Browne (4), Farrar (6) and Kelly (1); Martyn Hill and Michael George share the singing with Stephen Varcoe).

9. *Love Blows as the Wind Blows*

(a) Robert Tear (tenor), City of Birmingham Symphony Orchestra/Vernon Handley, HMV ASD 3896 (LP; cassette TC-ASD 3896), September 1980 (recorded 5–6 November 1979) (with Vaughan Williams, *On Wenlock Edge* and songs by Elgar).

(b) Stephen Varcoe (baritone), City of London Sinfonia/Richard Hickox, Chandos CHAN 8743 (for details of couplings, cf. 6(t)).

(c) Martin Oxenham (baritone), Bingham String Quartet, Duo DUOCD 89026 (with Walford Davies, *Prospice*; Somervell, *A Broken Arc*; Geoffrey Bush, *Farewell, Earth's Bliss*; Vaughan Williams, *Five Mystical Songs*).

10. *Folk Songs from Sussex*

Graham Trew (baritone), Roger Vignoles (piano), Hyperion A66037 (LP). May 1982 (recorded June 1981) (three songs only: 'A lawyer he went out', 'Roving in the dew', 'The true lover's farewell') (for details of couplings, *cf.* 4.)

BIBLIOGRAPHY

ALLEN, HUGH, 'George Butterworth and his Work', *Times Literary Supplement*, Vol. 797, p. 201, 26 April 1917.

ANGUS-BUTTERWORTH, LIONEL, *Sir Alex. K. Butterworth, Ll.B., and Captain G. S. K. Butterworth, M.C., B.A.*, Belfield Papers No. 5, 1979 (private publication).

ANON., *George Butterworth – The Man and His Music*, BBC Home Service, 14 July 1942: BBC Symphony Orchestra, led by Marie Wilson, conducted by Sir Adrian Boult; Henry Cummings (baritone), John Wills (piano); voices of Reginald Lennard, Sir Adrian Boult and Elizabeth Poston who, with Roger Fiske, devised the programme.

ARMSTRONG, SIR THOMAS, Introduction to the miniature score of the Rhapsody: *A Shropshire Lad*, Eulenburg, London 1981.

BAILEY, CYRIL, *Hugh Percy Allen*, Oxford University Press, Oxford and London, 1948.

BANFIELD, STEPHEN, 'On Interpreting Housman', *The British Music Society Newsletter*, No. 9, April 1981, pp. 4–11 (also in *Sensibility and English Song*, Vol. 2, pp. 400–5).

——, *Sensibility and English Song* (2 vols.), Cambridge University Press, Cambridge, 1985, paperback edn. 1989.

BARLOW, MICHAEL, 'George Butterworth: The Early Years', *Journal of the British Music Society*, Vol. 5, 1983, pp. 89–100.

——, 'George Butterworth and the Folksong Revival', *English Dance and Song*, Vol. 47, No. 3, Autumn/Winter 1985, pp. 10–11.

BAYLISS, STANLEY, 'George Butterworth, An Appreciation', *Musical Mirror*, August 1930, pp. 212 and 228.

——, 'Housman and the Composer', *The Listener*, Vol. XXIII, 11 April 1940, p. 756.

BIRD, JOHN, *Percy Grainger*, Elek Books, London, 1976; paperback edn. Faber and Faber, London, 1982.

BOUGHTON, RUTLAND, 'Modern British Song-writers. IV – George Butterworth', *Music Student*, December 1913, pp. 85–86.

BOULT, SIR ADRIAN, 'Butterworth', in Martin Anderson (ed.), *Boult on Music*, Toccata Press, London, 1983.

BOYD, A. K., *The History of Radley College, 1847–1947*, Blackwell, Oxford, 1948.

BUTCHER, VERNON, 'A. E. Housman and the English Composer', *Music & Letters*, Vol. XXIX, No. 4, October 1948, pp. 329–39.

BUTTERWORTH, SIR ALEXANDER (compiler), *Scrapbook of Letters, etc. concerning George Butterworth, 1903–1922*, Bodleian MS. Eng. misc. c.453.

—— (ed.), *George Butterworth, 1885–1916 (Memorial Volume)*. York and London, 1918, re-issued 1948 (both private publications). A valuable document, comprising a memoir by R. O. Morris, Butterworth's War Diary, letters, appreciations, and concert reviews. Only 100 copies of the original edition were printed.

BUTTERWORTH, MAY, *Alexander Kaye Butterworth, 1854–1946* (privately printed, n.d.). A memoir by a niece of Sir Alexander, it was presented to Cecil Sharp House in 1968, the year of her death.

COPLEY, IAN, *George Butterworth*, Thames Publishing, London, 1985.

CUDWORTH, 'CHARLES' (CYRIL), 'The "Shropshire Lad" and English Music', *Music*, Vol. I, November 1952, pp. 11–14.

DAUBNEY, BRIAN BLYTH, 'A Range of Hills', *British Music*, Vol. II, 1989, pp. 7–18.

DAWNEY, MICHAEL, 'George Butterworth's Folk Music Manuscripts'. *Folk Music Journal*, Vol. 3, No. 2, 1976, pp. 99–113.

—— (ed.), *The Ploughboy's Glory*, English Folk Dance and Song Society, London, 1977 (30 'hitherto unpublished' folk songs collected by Butterworth).

FOREMAN, LEWIS, *From Parry to Britten: British Music in Letters 1900–1945*, Batsford, London, 1987.

GAMMON, VIC, 'Folk-song Collecting in Sussex and Surrey, 1843–1914', *History Workshop Journal*, Vol. 10, Autumn 1980, pp. 61–89.

GRACE, HARVEY, 'Butterworth and the Folksong Revival', *The Listener*, Vol. xxviii, No. 704, 9 July 1942, p. 61.

GRAVES, RICHARD PERCEVAL, *A. E. Housman – The Scholar-Poet*, Routledge and Kegan Paul, London, 1979; Oxford University Press, Oxford and London, 1981.

HEANEY, MIKE, 'Butterworth Dancing', *The Morris Dancer*, No. 15, March 1983, pp. 7–12.

——, 'Films from the Past', *English Dance and Song*, Vol. 45, No. 3, Autumn/Winter 1983, pp. 20–1.

HEATH-COLEMAN, PHILIP, 'Morris Dancing at Filkins', *English Dance and Song*, Vol. 44, No. 1, Spring 1982, pp. 14–16.

HOWES, FRANK, 'Letters to Clive Carey', *English Dance and Song*, Vol. 33, No. 2, Summer 1971, pp. 65–66.

HULL, ROBERT, 'A Bibliography of the Settings of Poems from "A

Shropshire Lad" and "Last Poems" by A. E. Housman', *Dominant*, February 1928, pp. 26–9.

——, 'George Butterworth', *Musical Opinion*, December 1932, pp. 212–13, and January 1933, pp. 310–11.

JUDGE, ROY, 'Mary Neal and the Espérance Morris', *Folk Music Journal*, Vol. 5, No. 5, 1989, pp. 545–91.

KARPELES, MAUD, *Cecil Sharp, His Life and Work*, Routledge and Kegan Paul, London, 1967.

KEEL, FREDERICK, (ed.), *Journal of the Folk-Song Society*, Vol. 4, No. 15, December 1910; and Vol. 4, No. 17, January 1913.

KENNEDY, DOUGLAS, 'Cecil Sharp 1911–24', *The Morris Dancer*, No. 4, August 1979, pp. 16–18.

——, 'Recollections', *The Morris Dancer*, No. 12, March 1982, pp. 6–9.

——, 'Tradition', *Folk Music Journal*, Vol. 4, No. 3, 1982, pp. 195–207.

KENNEDY, MICHAEL, *The Works of Ralph Vaughan Williams*, Oxford University Press, Oxford and London, 1964, paperback edn. 1971, 2nd edn. 1980.

——, *Adrian Boult*, Hamish Hamilton, London, 1987.

LLOYD, A. L., *Folk Song and the Collectors*, BBC Radio 3, 26 September 1983.

LOCKSPEISER, EDWARD, 'Mixed Gallery', in A. L. Bacharach (ed.), *British Music of Our Time*, Pelican Books, London, 1946, pp. 192–93.

LUCAS, EDWARD VERRALL, *London Lavender*, Methuen, London, 1912, pp. 220–24.

NEWMAN, ERNEST, 'Concerning "A Shropshire Lad" and Other Matters', *The Musical Times*, Vol. lix, September 1918, pp. 393–8.

——, 'Mr. Housman and the Composers', *The Sunday Times*, 29 October 1922, p. 7.

PALMER, CHRISTOPHER, 'Butterworth, George (Sainton Kaye)', in Stanley Sadie (ed.), *The New Grove Dictionary of Music and Musicians*, Macmillan, London, 1980, Vol. 3, pp. 521–22.

PIRIE, PETER, Introduction to *Eleven Songs from 'A Shropshire Lad'*, by *George Butterworth*, Stainer and Bell, London, 1974, pp. ii–iii.

——, Introduction to *Folk Songs from Sussex and Other Songs by George Butterworth*, Stainer and Bell, London, 1974, pp. ii–iii.

QUINLAN, JOHN, 'A. E. Housman and British Composers', *The Musical Times*, Vol. c., No. 1393, March 1959, pp. 137–38.

RANKIN, A. C., 'George Jerrard Wilkinson', *The British Music Society Newsletter*, No. 4, Winter 1979, pp. 9–11.

RIPPIN, JOHN, 'George Butterworth 1885–1916', *The Musical Times*, Vol. cvii, No. 1483, August 1966, pp. 680–82; and No. 1484, September 1966, pp. 769–71.

SCHOFIELD, DEREK, ' "Revival of the Folk Dance: An Artistic Movement": The Background to the Founding of the English Folk Dance Society in 1911', *Folk Music Journal*, Vol. 5, No. 2, 1986, pp. 215–19.

SYMONS, KATHERINE, correspondence on 'A. E. Housman and music', *Music & Letters*, Vol. XXV, No. 1, January 1944, pp. 60–61.

THOMPSON, KENNETH, 'A Butterworth Catalogue', *The Musical Times*, Vol. cvii, No. 1484, September 1966, pp. 771–72.

VAUGHAN WILLIAMS, RALPH, 'Chapter of Musical Autobiography', in Hubert Foss, *Ralph Vaughan Williams: A Study*, Harrap, London, 1950, pp. 18–38; reprinted in (a) Ralph Vaughan Williams, *Some Thoughts on Beethoven's Choral Symphony, with Writings on Other Musical Subjects*, Oxford University Press, Oxford and London, 1953, pp. 132–58, (b) Ralph Vaughan Williams, *National Music and Other Essays*, Oxford University Press, Oxford and London, 1963 (2nd edn. 1987), pp. 177–94.

VAUGHAN WILLIAMS, URSULA, *R. V. W.: A Portrait of Ralph Vaughan Williams*, Oxford University Press, Oxford and London, 1964; paperback edn. 1988.

WELLS-HARRISON, W., 'Some Notable British Music, V – George Butterworth: Songs from "A Shropshire Lad" ', *The Musical Standard*, 29 July 1916, p. 81.

WHITE, WILLIAM, 'A. E. Housman and Music', *Music & Letters*, Vol. XXIV, No. 4, October 1943, pp. 208–19.

WORTLEY, RUSSELL, 'The Bucknell Morris', *English Dance and Song*, Vol. 41, No. 2, 1979, pp. 12–14.

WORTLEY, RUSSELL, and DAWNEY, MICHAEL (eds.), 'George Butterworth's Diary of Morris Dance Hunting', *Folk Music Journal*, Vol. 3, No. 3, 1977, pp. 193–207.

Index
of Butterworth's Music

Index
of Folksongs and Dances

General
Index

Numbers in italics indicate illustrations